"Even though Dietrich Bonhoeffer is dead, like Abel, he still speaks. In *Letter to the American Church*, Eric Metaxas has given him a megaphone. We would do well to heed this five-bell alarm."

> **—Anne Graham Lotz,** author of eleven books, including *Just Give Me Jesus*

"This book is like a bucket of cold water thrown into the face of a sleeping church. I found myself arguing with Eric over some points, but I was struck with the uncanny parallels he draws between the compliant churches in Nazi Germany and our churches today. If you are inclined to think you might disagree with what he has to say, here is my challenge: read this book and ask yourself, 'Where does Eric have it wrong?' I think you will find that question more difficult to answer than you expected. I personally think this is Eric Metaxas's most important book for us today."

> **—Erwin W. Lutzer,** pastor emeritus, The Moody Church, Chicago

"Eric Metaxas has spent years researching and writing about giants of our faith; from that wealth of insight and understanding he has taken a new step. In *Letter to the American Church*, he has issued a call to action. The message is historically informed, biblically sound, and—I believe—'Spirit-directed.' I pray every Christian in our nation will take the time to read and consider what Eric has presented."

> **—Allen Jackson,** senior pastor of World Outreach Church, Murfreesboro, Tennessee

"Back in the 60s when I escaped with my life from the socialist dictatorship of President Nasser of Egypt, I only wanted to come to America. Why America? Because its system of government has never been duplicated. The founders ensured that the ultimate authority under

God is not the President, nor the Congress, but 'We the people.' Thus, they drafted the greatest political document in all human history, the U.S. Constitution. Yet many of my fellow pastors who claim to relevantly and contextually interpret the word of God fail to take this 'unique' blessing of 'We the people' as the governing authority to heart. They sold out this blessing and exchanged it for selective silence against the modern scourge of the evils of wokeness. Nay, some of them even baptized this evil into their church's catechism. Unbeknownst to them, they are handing over the keys of their own freedom to preach the Gospel to the enemy of their souls. Perhaps there is no modern writer who can draw the comparison of this selective silence on the part of many American pastors to the German church in the 1920s and 1930s like Eric Metaxas. In the pages of this book you now hold in your hands, there is a solemn warning. Read it and heed it and pass it on to many others."

> **—Michael Youssef,** Ph.D., senior pastor of the Church of the Apostles in Atlanta, Georgia, and executive president of Leading the Way

"This is a bold and insightful book with a deeply troubling message. Eric Metaxas calls for pastors (and other Christian leaders) who, like Bonhoeffer in Germany in the 1930s, will be courageous enough to speak unambiguously against the massive anti-Christian forces that now threaten to permanently transform American society and bring to an end America's role as a beacon of freedom for the world."

> **—Wayne Grudem,** distinguished research professor of theology and biblical studies, Phoenix Seminary

"A prophetic trumpet blast warning of the parallels between the darkness of a previous era and the coming darkness of our own, *Letter to the American Church* lingers in the chambers of the heart and pleads with the hearer to reckon with this message of a modern watchman on the wall."

> **—David Engelhardt,** senior pastor of Kings' Church NYC and author of *Good Kills*

Letter to the American Church

Letter

to the

American
Church

Eric Metaxas

AUTHOR OF ***BONHOEFFER: PASTOR, MARTYR, PROPHET, SPY***

SALEM
BOOKS

an imprint of Regnery Publishing
Washington, D.C.

Salem Books™ is a trademark of Salem Communications Holding Corporation. Regnery® is a registered trademark and its colophon is a trademark of Salem Communications Holding Corporation.

Cataloging-in-Publication data on file with the Library of Congress

ISBN: 978-1-68451-389-5
eISBN: 978-1-68451-390-1

Library of Congress Control Number: 2022937954

Published in the United States by
Salem Books
An Imprint of Regnery Publishing
A Division of Salem Media Group
Washington, D.C.
www.SalemBooks.com

Manufactured in the United States of America

10 9 8 7 6

Books are available in quantity for promotional or premium use. For information on discounts and terms, please visit our website: www.SalemBooks.com.

Contents

Introduction

I have written this book because I am convinced the American Church is at an impossibly—and almost unbearably—important inflection point. The parallels to where the German Church was in the 1930s are unavoidable and grim. So the only question—and what concerns us in this slim volume—is whether we might understand those parallels, and thereby avoid the fatal mistakes the German Church made during that time, and their superlatively catastrophic results. If we do not, I am convinced we will reap a whirlwind greater even than the one they did.

The German Church of the 1930s was silent in the face of evil; but can there be any question whether the American Church of our own time is guilty of the same silence? Because of this, I am compelled to speak out, and to say what—only by God's grace—I might say to make plain where we find ourselves at this moment, at our own unavoidably crucial crossroads in history.

�֍

It is for good or for ill that America plays an inescapably central role in the world. If you have not read Alexis de Tocqueville on this subject, you likely nonetheless understand that the extent to which that central role has been used for good and for God's purposes has had everything to do with our churches, or with the American Church, as we may call her. So if America is in any way exceptional, it has nothing to do with the blood that runs through American veins and everything to do with the blood shed for us on Calvary, and the extent to which we have acknowledged this. America has led the world in making religious liberty paramount, knowing that is only with a deep regard for it that we may speak of liberty at all. It was this that made Tocqueville marvel most: that while in other nations—and especially in his own nation of France—the Church was adamantly opposed to the idea of political liberty, in America it was the churches that helped encourage, create, and sustain a culture of liberty.

Because of the outsized role America plays in the world today, the importance of whether we learn the lesson of what happened to the German Church ninety years ago cannot be overstated. Though it may be a gruesome thing to consider, the monstrous evil that befell the civilized world precisely because of the German Church's failure is likely a mere foretaste of what will befall the world if the American Church fails in a similar way at this hour.

And at present we are indeed failing.

We should underscore the idea that the centrality of our nation in the world does not mean that we are intrinsically exceptional, but rather that God has sovereignly chosen us to hold the torch of liberty for all the world, and that the Church is central to our doing this. So the idea that He has charged us with this most solemn duty should make us tremble. Nonetheless, we must carry out that duty in a way that is the opposite of prideful and that is meant to be an invitation to all beyond our shores. If we should aspire—in the words of Jesus as quoted by John Winthrop—to be a "shining city on a hill," the idea is that we should exist and shine for the sake of others and not for ourselves alone. President Abraham Lincoln said that we in America were God's "almost chosen people," and acknowledged that this placed upon us an almost unbearable burden. It is a certainty from the Scriptures and from our experience over the centuries that apart from God we can do nothing. So if God has chosen us for some task, we must do all we can to shoulder that task, and must know more than anything that unless we lean on Him and acknowledge Him in all our ways, we are guaranteed to fail.

We must also remind ourselves that when God chooses anyone—whether the nation of Israel or a single person—to perform any role or any task, it is never something to be celebrated, as though the one chosen has won a contest. Quite to the contrary: it is a grave and fearsome responsibility. So if the Lord has chosen America and the American Church to stand against the evils and deceptions of this present darkness, we had better be sure we understand what is required of us, and had better make sure we do all that is possible to fulfill our charge.

Throughout this book I will touch on some of the issues we are facing, but let us here say that it is something almost unprecedented: the emergence of ideas and forces that ultimately are at war with God Himself. It's easy to see this with regard to Germany in the 1930s, when we think of the death camps and the murder of so many millions, but we need to understand that in the beginning they had no idea where it was leading, and had no idea they were facing nothing less than the forces of anti-Christ. We are now facing those same forces in different guises. But the extent of it is even worse than it was ninety years ago, because those forces do not have an agenda that is hyper-nationalistic, as in Germany, but that is actually anti-nationalistic—which is to say that it is globalist.

These ideas seem to have emerged lately, but they have been growing quietly in our midst and we have not taken them seriously enough. Many have been fooled into thinking them essentially harmless. We are today like the proverbial frog in the saucepan, simmering along and never realizing that unless we see our situation and leap out now, we are very soon to be cooked and beyond all leaping. The ideas and forces we face have an atheistic Marxist ideology in common, although it never declares itself as such. It knows that doing this would wake many people up who are still asleep, and that would ruin everything.

But what we must dare to see is that these many ideas share a bitter taproot that leads all the way down to Hell. Critical Race Theory—which is atheistic and Marxist—and radical transgender and pro-abortion ideologies are all inescapably anti-God and anti-human. So they are dedicatedly at war with the ideas of family and marriage, and with the idea of America as a force for good—as a force for spreading the Gospel and Gospel values throughout the world. These ideas have over many decades infiltrated our own culture in such a way that they touch everything, and part of what makes them so wicked is that they smilingly pretend to share the biblical values that champion the underdog against the oppressor. As Stalin and Hitler and Mao would butcher millions in the name of fighting for "the people," so these forces do the same and are angling to do much, much more of the same—if we will allow them the time to strengthen themselves, if we do not fight with all our might and main against them right now.

One of the principal ways in which they have gained strength is in persuading so many in the American Church that to fight them is to abandon the "Gospel" for pure culture warring or for politics. This is not just nonsense, but is a supremely deceptive and satanic lie, designed only to silence those who would genuinely speak for truth.

So those who behave as though there is really nothing to worry about, who seem to think—as such prominent pastors as Andy Stanley and others do—that we ought to assiduously avoid fighting these threats and be "apolitical" are tragically mistaken, are burying their heads in the sand and exhorting others to do the same. Or to put it another way, they are in their churches singing more and more loudly to drown out the cries of those in the boxcars heading to their gruesome deaths. Sing with us, they say, and don't worry about all of those other issues out there. They don't concern us. Our job is to focus on God, and to pretend that we can do so without fighting for those He loves, whose lives and futures are being destroyed.

✼

So to restate our situation, this is not a task or duty we in the American Church have asked for. Nonetheless, just as the German Church had a painfully important task and did not rise to that occasion to perform it, so we have a painfully important task, whether we have asked for it or not. God calls us to do something, but the choice whether we do it is entirely ours. Because we are made in God's image, we are perfectly free, and therefore cannot be compelled to do what is right. It is a chilling prospect, especially in light of the failure of the German Church.

If anyone would feel that believing God has chosen the American Church for such a vital role somehow smacks of an egotistical nationalism, they have already bought into the Marxist and globalist lie that America is nothing special—or is probably a force for evil at this point. In any case, they miss the point and have only leapt away from one ditch to fall headlong into another. It is a fact that God in His sovereignty chose the German Church to stand against the evils of its day, but it shrank from acknowledging this and from standing.

Germany has been living with the deep shame over it unto this day. So for the American Church to say that God has not chosen us is as bad as saying He must choose us because we deserve to be chosen. Both stances are equally guilty of the sin of pride. It is far easier to ignore God's call than to acknowledge it and rise to fulfill it, but it is more difficult and painful than anything to live with the results of ignoring God's call. Let the reader understand.

Chapter One

What Is the Church?

"See, I have set before you today life and good, death and evil. If you obey the commandments of the Lord your God that I command you today, by loving the Lord your God, by walking in his ways, and by keeping his commandments and his statutes and his rules, then you shall live and multiply, and the Lord your God will bless you in the land that you are entering to take possession of it. But if your heart turns away, and you will not hear, but are drawn away to worship other gods and serve them, I declare to you today, that you shall surely perish. You shall not live long in the land that you are going over the Jordan to enter and possess. I call heaven and earth to witness against you today, that I have set before you life and death, blessing and curse. Therefore choose life, that you and your offspring may live, loving the Lord your God, obeying his voice and holding fast to him, for he is your life and length of days, that you may dwell in the land that the Lord swore to your fathers, to Abraham, to Isaac, and to Jacob, to give them."

—DEUTERONOMY 30:15–20

Before we explore the parallels of our situation and choices to those of the German Church in the 1930s, we must briefly touch upon the American Church of our own time. In doing so, we cannot go very far without raising the most fundamental question:

What is the Church?

The Christian martyr Dietrich Bonhoeffer asked and answered that question in his brilliant doctoral dissertation, *Sanctorum Communio,* written when he was only twenty-one years old. But much

1

more importantly, he continued to ask and answer that question with his very life, until his untimely death eighteen years later at the hands of the Nazi regime. The question was not, and could not only be, academic or theological or intellectual. In some ways, it is the most fundamental question in human existence.

If the God of the Bible is real, if He created the universe and created us and sent His Son to die and rise again so that we might have a relationship with Him now and for all eternity, there cannot possibly be any more important question. What does it mean for those of us who would say we are Christians to be Christians? What exactly is the Church, which God tells us is His Bride?

Some might say the Church is a movement or an institution, but that is hardly God's idea about what the Church is or is supposed to be. The real question is more pointed: When is the Church actually *being* the Church of Jesus Christ, instead of being that in name only? In the Old Testament God sent prophets to call the people of God *actually to be the people of God*, not only in name, but in how they lived. And in the last two thousand years God has sent prophetic figures to do the same thing: to call the people of God—what we now know as the Church—*actually to be the Church.*

Dietrich Bonhoeffer was one of those voices. He called the German Church actually to *be* the Church in their time and, as I hope to make clear, his voice to them is his voice to us today, calling the American Church to actually *be* God's church, with all that entails, so that we might avoid the mistakes of the German Church in the 1930s, and those direst consequences we know to have been their result. But let's face it: what God usually asks of His people is that they actually live out their faith in all the spheres of their lives so that all of society is blessed. And when they fail to do this, they are failing to be the Church.

So when we ask what the Church is today—and consider the condition of the Church today—we should first admit that in latter decades it has receded more and more from public life. In many ways, instead of taking the Church out into the world—and blessing the world—it has shrunk backward into what it mistakenly thinks of as a proper "religious" sphere. This seems to be its misguided way of apologizing for perhaps having been too political in the 1980s and 1990s, when the "Moral Majority" and "Religious Right" were the bogeyman of the secular media, who always accused Christians of being too "political," as they do today when anything we might say nettles their own uncompromising secular doctrines. But many in the churches were not up to these criticisms, and weary of the contentious culture wars, they thought that yes, perhaps it was time to retreat to strictly "theological" and "religious" issues. Perhaps it was time merely to "preach the Gospel"—as though such a thing were logically possible, as though the Gospel ever could be kept from touching upon all of the issues of human life. Or as though that would be anything but an abdication of God's calling.

The sociologist James Davison Hunter became for many the voice of this approach which, in his 2010 book *To Change the World*, he referred to as "Faithful Presence." For many, this came to mean that we in the Church ought not to be too bold about what we believe and proclaim. Perhaps it would just be wiser to keep a bit quiet and to be Christians in a way that was not very actively engaged with the world around us, but that might have an effect over the long term.

But the God who Himself *is* Truth cannot under any circumstances be chased into some arbitrary "religious" corner, as though the Church's witness in the public square is somehow inherently untoward and overly aggressive. Nor can Christians be forced to express their faith only on Sunday mornings and only in certain buildings. Those who purport to call Him Lord can never allow themselves to go along with whatever such contorted theological calisthenics would involve. Such a view is at its core simply secular, and constitutes a fundamental misunderstanding of who God is. Nonetheless many Christians—often for understandable if mistaken reasons—have gone along with this, somehow thinking it to be the best way forward.

The first thing to be said about this—to the extent anyone has gone along with such views—is that we hope they might see their error and repent. It is in brutal atheistic regimes like China where such attitudes can be seen to prevail in all of their horror, where the state insists upon such a view and has the power to enforce it, essentially saying, "You may do as you like in that building at such and such hours, but when you come out you must bow to the secular authority of the state." In America we have usually understood things dramatically differently. We have known that religious liberty means we are not merely able to worship privately, and to keep our religion to ourselves, but are guaranteed a "free exercise thereof," so that our faith must by definition be carried everywhere we go, on every day of the week and in every place we take ourselves. Many have died for these freedoms, so the mistaken idea that we should voluntarily give them up is unprecedented, deeply un-American, and cannot be allowed to continue. It constitutes a violation of the most central idea of what makes America America.

But where did we ever get the idea that we should mind our own business along such lines, as though the truth of God were a parochial, subjective idea that had no bearing on anything beyond our private prayer times and churches? Where did we who claim to be the Church ever get the idea that we shouldn't express any number of things too loudly, that we shouldn't—for example—express the biblical view of human sexuality as a sacred and mysterious bond which God created only for the marriage between men and women for life? Where did we get the idea that we don't have an obligation to tell the world what God says about such things—about the unborn and about human freedom and human rights? Or about anything, including the deadly perniciousness of Marxist atheist philosophy, whether in eco-nomics or in any other sphere? Where did we get the idea that we shouldn't be at the forefront in criticizing the great evil of Communist countries like China that brutally persecute religious minorities in ways that bring to mind the Nazis themselves? And why would we not speak out against American and international corporations that do business with them until they force them to take human rights seriously and change their inhuman practices? How dare we be silent about such things?

We must remember that William Wilberforce in his day was told to keep his faith private, and was told that his "religious" view that slavery was wrong had no business poking out into the wide world. It was thought an absolute scandal that a man would bring his religion into the public sphere and dare to impose his views through the laws of the land. But Wilberforce knew that his "religious" views about slavery were only "religious" to those who didn't like them, many of whom were making monstrous profits from the evil of the transat-lantic slave trade. So we thank God that he did not let those naysayers dissuade him one bit and kept at his campaign to end slavery, having no doubt that it was God's will for him to do so. He also had no doubt that it was the duty of everyone who dared identify as a member of the Church in England to join him in this, and to that extent was a prophetic voice to the Church of his time. But where are those voices in the American Church today regarding the inhuman cruelties per-petrated by the Chinese Communists on the Uyghur Muslims and so many others?

Of course, Dietrich Bonhoeffer too was told not to be "political." His Christian faith gave him the idea that because German Jews were being wickedly persecuted he had an obligation to speak out, and not only to speak out but to do everything he could—unto the point of surrendering his own life—for what he knew to be right. He understood that what is right and true is never merely right and true for some, but is inevitably right and true for all—or is not right and true at all. So Bonhoeffer dared to call upon his fellow church leaders to stand with him in these things. But early on in this effort, he saw that his was an increasingly lonely path, and that eventually he would be virtually alone with God in pursuing what he believed was right.

So the question comes to us: How is it that so many in the American Church of our time have shrunk back from public engagement, and quietly assented to the decidedly unbiblical—and decidedly un-American and unconstitutional—view that the truth of God is not applicable beyond the churches? How have we been persuaded to be silent in the face of evil? When did we begin to agree with those trying so hard to marginalize our views, to think that perhaps they had a point, and perhaps we shouldn't express our views too vigorously, lest we be accused of trying to impose them on the rest of the culture? If Wilberforce did not let the pro-slavery voices of his day deter him and Bonhoeffer did not let the pro-Nazi voices of his day deter him, why have so many American church leaders let the voices of their ideological opponents cow them into silence? Do we not realize that no good ever can come of such silence and inaction, that human beings whom God loves suffer when His own people fail to express boldly what He has said and when they fail to live as He has called them to live?

So how in the world did the current situation come about?

✳

The late, great Chuck Colson rarely gave a speech in which he did not quote a certain statement of the Dutch statesman and theologian Abraham Kuyper. "There is not one square inch," Kuyper said in 1880, "in the whole domain of our human existence over which Christ, who is Sovereign, does not cry 'Mine!'" Kuyper himself, in being both a statesman and a theologian, obviously lived out this idea. Thinking we would keep our faith in some religious or theological corner is—as we say—preposterous. But the reason Colson quoted Kuyper as often as he did was because the contrary idea had begun to find purchase in some Christian circles.

Part of this may be traced back to the 1960s, when the U.S. Supreme Court took prayer out of the public schools—but the problem is less this specific action than what it represented and portended. It was part of a general trend down a path that was fundamentally mistaken in its views of Jefferson's famous "wall of separation" between church and state. Rather than protecting people of faith from government intrusion, as the Founders intended—which is of course the central idea of what we call religious liberty—the judiciary instead began to interpret it to mean that the public square should be stripped of faith entirely. The Reverend Richard John Neuhaus famously called this the creation of "the naked public square,"[1] which was the perfect opposite of the Founders' intentions. And it must be said emphatically that to secularize the public square is actually to impose upon it a religion of another kind, albeit in a way that very cleverly and dishonestly pretends not to be religious at all. But on matters that touch on the fundamentals of human existence, especially with regard to such institutions as marriage and the sanctity of life, we are inescapably dealing with religious issues. So to stand against the views of people of faith is—quite ironically but unavoidably—to take a distinctly "religious" view nonetheless, and to seek to impose it. And so the Supreme Court and the federal government, which are expressly forbidden from putting a thumb on the scales—but who are to allow the American people to exercise their wills and to have freedom in all things—began to impose secular views. The

---

[1] In 1984 he wrote a book with that title, *The Naked Public Square: Religion and Democracy in America*.

justices did this most infamously when in 1973 they purported to discover in the Constitution a "right to abortion," where of course none existed or ever could exist. In the decades since that time, they continued to drift farther beyond their ordained judicial orbit and have sometimes legislated unconstitutionally from the bench. So because the American people did not sufficiently see the dangers of this, and because Christian leaders did not speak out boldly, the drift toward an unconstitutional and secular view began to be enshrined in our laws and in our culture.

We must also go back to the mid-1950s to understand what happened. It was in 1954 that then-Senator Lyndon Johnson introduced an amendment to the U.S. tax code prohibiting churches—and any other nonprofit organizations—from taking a public stand on political candidates. If anyone from a pulpit dared to endorse a candidate, that church's tax exemption would be repealed. It is astonishing that pastors in America allowed this wild idea to go uncontested. In this they behaved rather like many of the submissive pastors in Germany two decades earlier. Of course, for American pastors to submit meekly to anything like this is far more shocking, given our own history of religious liberty and freedom of speech.

As a result of these and other events, a pall was cast over many churches, and faith over time began to be "privatized"—to recede from the public sphere and from being applied to issues that went beyond mere theology and personal pietism; and this erroneous view became increasingly normalized. But it is an inescapable and painful fact: if the churches in America are not free to speak on any topic and in any way that they choose—and if they voluntarily go along with this view—then no one in America is truly free, and America herself has effectively ceased to exist.

We have to see just how outrageous it is that this has indeed happened. How could the government in putting forth the so-called

"Johnson Amendment" dare to draw any lines around what could be said in a sermon—in which God's own Word is to be delivered? What could conceivably be more deserving of complete freedom than that form—of all forms—of public speech? And if the conscience of the man of God in that pulpit would cause him to speak for or against a candidate, what is that to the U.S. government? In fact, it is none of its business.

Have we forgotten that pastors in the eighteenth century spoke boldly from their colonial pulpits against the tyranny of King George III, and opposed him by name? Was it not their voices that helped us to gain our freedoms and that helped us to create a Constitution in which all of our freedoms were enshrined in a way that has been the envy of the whole world ever since? Were pastors from their American pulpits in the nineteenth century not allowed to speak against those candidates who expressed racist and pro-slavery views? Did they not even have an obligation to educate their congregations on such things and to encourage them to choose leaders who shared God's views? Finally, were pastors in the twentieth century not allowed to speak out against candidates who advocated for Jim Crow laws? Do we think they ought to have been?

This is no way for any Christian—much less a pastor—to parse what he may be "allowed" to say, and certainly not from the pulpit. It can only be God—and our consciences guided by Him—that can determine what we should and shouldn't say. So our total freedom—in and beyond our pulpits—is nonnegotiable. The truth cannot be contained, and certainly not in categories that have been arbitrarily chosen and defined by others. So when did these pernicious ideas come into American churches?

Perhaps the more important question is: why did Christian leaders submit to these un-Christian and un-American ideas? And why are they submitting to them today? Have so many pastors today really forgotten that it is God who calls them to their posts, and God who fills their churches and keeps them filled? Have they forgotten what the Scriptures say: that if they honor God, He will honor them? Has keeping an eye on the bottom line and on the numbers in attendance caused them to drift away from the very reason God called them to the pulpit in the first place? Have they become like the leaders of American corporations, who have become especially cowardly and seem willing to say and do whatever someone advises them is necessary to avoid trouble and keep them from being "cancelled"?

Have the blessings we have in America made us so comfortable and so soft that we have forgotten that God expects us to serve Him with everything we have, and that if we are in leadership, He requires us to understand that our greater position of authority comes with even greater expectations? Of course, many American pastors probably never had this kind of heroic faith to begin with. And there are some who once had it, but who over time have lost their first love and drifted to that awful point at which they are in danger of judgment, just as the German Christians in the 1930s and just as the Christians in Ephesus in the first century were.

Will those among us who have lost our first love repent before it's too late?

✳

There are a host of reasons—and excuses—for the behavior of many pastors and Christian leaders, and we will touch on them as we go forward because many of them are the same reasons and excuses given by German pastors in the 1930s. But the language of many contemporary American Christians is different than that of the German pastors of the 1930s in one principal respect. The American Christians of our own time have taken to using the term "the Gospel" in a new way, as though by doing this they hope to set religious and theological issues apart from all else, as though this were possible. And so now, when many American church leaders shrink from taking a particular stand, they often say that they are doing so "for the sake of the Gospel." It is "for the sake of the Gospel" that we will not contest these things, they say, that we will assiduously avoid taking sides in these terribly divisive "culture wars," and will even more assiduously avoid being identified with any political party or candidate. The idea is that anything that might conceivably be accused of "being political" is manifestly out of bounds.

But how can we have come to this bizarre pass? If there are injustices done to our fellow Americans, are we not to protest and, if necessary, even fight politically for what is right, just as Bonhoeffer and Wilberforce did? When is speaking against injustice "merely political"? And when and how did "Gospel-related" issues retreat to where they can only be those issues of justice that fall on one side of the political spectrum? Are we to be hoodwinked so easily? Who decided that being political means we are not being "Gospel"-oriented?

Part of the problem is that times have changed. As James R. Wood well describes in a recent article in *First Things* magazine, titled "How I Evolved on Tim Keller," the problem is not at all that wonderful pastors like New York's Tim Keller were wrong in their assessments that we should avoid politics and culture-warring, but that as circumstances in our own culture changed, they eventually became wrong by sticking to a script that was no longer right for the time in which we found ourselves. Woods writes:

> Keller's "third way" philosophy has serious limitations as a framework for moral reasoning as well. Too often it encourages in its adherents a pietistic impulse to keep one's hands clean, stay above the fray, and at a distance from

imperfect options for addressing complex social and political issues. It can also produce conflict-aversion, and thus it is instinctively accommodating. By always giving equal airtime to the flaws in every option, the third-way posture can also give the impression that the options are equally bad, failing to sufficiently recognize ethical asymmetry.

As a result of such thinking, many have continued to believe that the approaches to the culture that worked in 1995 or 2005 must still work today. How one wishes that were true. But what worked then does not and cannot work anymore; and we are obliged to face this, just as the German Church was obliged to see that what worked under the Kaisers would not work under Adolf Hitler. The circumstances have changed, and we must adjust.

Of course, most Christian leaders have not seen the change and have not adjusted, but continue to act as though it is an unseemly betrayal of their calling to say anything that might open them to the accusation of being political. As we have mentioned, during the recent pandemic when churches were preposterously deemed "non-essential" by governors and mayors—while marijuana dispensaries and casinos and strip clubs remained open—many pastors behaved as though it was their Christian duty not to speak, as though this were the "winsome" way forward. When questionable medical procedures were being forced on their parishioners—some of which were manufactured with cells used from aborted babies—they meekly adopted the stance that it was the "Christ-like" thing to submit and not to fight, nor even to mention such tremendously serious issues. This was a deeply disgraceful moment for the American Church.

Believers have always been called to speak the truth and to fight against injustice of any kind. As we have said, we are obliged courageously to bring our faith to bear on all issues.

The Church is called to speak out and to fight not just when the cause is fashionable—as with such causes as human trafficking—but also when it is unfashionable, and perhaps especially when it is unfashionable. If we do nothing when we see our culture being attacked in ways that will cause innumerable people to suffer, will not God hold us accountable? We are responsible to those suffering now, and to those in future generations. How can we let others—rather than our own consciences—dictate what we say and do?

God expects those who have a voice to speak out for those who do not—who most of all tend to be the poorest among us. So if we as Christians see Marxist policies being proposed and enacted—which we certainly know may crush the poor into the dust for generations—shall we be silent lest someone accuse us of being political, or worse, "a member of the Religious Right"? Is that all it takes for the forces of evil to crush the poor in our time? If I know that Critical Race Theory will divide our nation horribly and will destroy the fabric of society, am I to keep silent because someone will cynically call me a racist for raising my concerns? To remain silent because some will call us names and criticize us is simply to be cowardly, and constitutes a simple failure to trust God.

And what if standing with the disenfranchised and the poor also means standing with those who are lower-class whites? Will we step aside from doing so because this is unfashionable in some circles, or because someone might cynically call us "white supremacists"? Will we refrain from standing up for people of color who don't toe the line of those who claim to represent them? We must once and forever stop pretending that speaking the truth on any of these issues means leaving the "Gospel" for politics and "culture warring." We must declare what we know to be true. And part of what we must declare is that the secular leftists in America—and leftists in the Church too—have become radically political and are cynically pretending that those who disagree with them are the ones being political. All truth is truth, and we are responsible to stand up and do what we can. What are we afraid of? If God be for us, who can be against us? Does that scripture no longer mean what it once did? If we believe God demands we speak the truth as we see it for His purposes, how have we so easily let ourselves be turned aside into silence?

Because of all these things, where we are now in America could hardly be more dire. In some ways it is as though George Orwell had scripted it, except it is far stranger than anything he ever wrote; as if a piñata in the shape of Karl Marx has been beaten asunder and a confetti of new words and impossible-to-fathom concepts has fallen over everything. Suddenly the false, confusing, and wicked ideas that come from Critical Theory and "Transgender and Queer Theory" have not only erupted into culture but have been welcomed into many churches, whose leaders seem not to understand that the cultural Marxism from which these ideas derive is inherently atheistic and dedicatedly opposed to the God they claim to represent and serve. These ideas can never accord with the reality and order of the world that God has created. The proponents of these ideas are in fact at war with God and God's reality, though of course they will hardly admit as much. But what concerns us far more than the cynical and confused proponents of these ideas is that many church leaders are afraid to stand against them. That is the central horror of our time.

What more needs to happen before Christian leaders see that things have changed? What more needs to happen for them to see that God calls them to stand and fight against the unfurling madness? Everywhere we see things we could not have imagined even a few years ago. Children have been subjected to unimaginably inappropriate ideas by teachers paid with our tax dollars, and their parents have even been told that their children's learning is no concern of theirs and that the state will choose what and how they learn. This is

Communism come to America. Can there be any other way to say it? Do we need to be reminded that no greater evangelist than Billy Graham himself spoke aggressively against Communism in the 1950s, knowing that it was the enemy of all God held dear—the enemy of God's people and of God Himself? If the one man most famous in America for evangelism and for preaching the pure Gospel of Christ felt the need to speak so very boldly against the evil of Communism, how can we today fail to do at least the same when its horrors are falling upon us and our children in such measures as Dr. Graham hardly could have conceived?

Nonetheless, we have seen how many churches and church leaders hold back from speaking or acting. As we have said, during the COVID-19 pandemic, political figures decreed that churches were to be shuttered, and that the spiritual health of Americans was meaningless. If ever there was a shot heard round the world in our own time, that was it. But how many rallied to that cause and said, "We are obliged to keep our churches open? Not because we don't care about the health of our parishioners, but precisely because we do, and because we know that their health is a more complicated thing than some are making it out to be. Our fidelity is to God, and we will bear whatever consequences may come. Here we stand, we can do no other." How many Christian leaders spoke out in that way?

Some stood heroically, but the overwhelming majority did not. Although American Christians genuinely look to their leaders to help them face the evils being unleashed on them and their neighbors, most pastors were and continue to be as silent as church mice. Why? Will some of them at last now wake up and repent? Will some at last now begin to speak up—or will they forever hold their peace and invite the judgment that is sure to come?

Chapter Two

Does God Ask Us to See the Future?

A s I have said, to understand where we are today in the American Church, we are obliged to see what happened to the Church in Germany in the 1930s. Because I became closely familiar with that subject in writing my biography of Dietrich Bonhoeffer,[1] I have been troubled and astonished by the growing parallels for some time.

Most American Christians have some idea of the tragic blindness of the Church in Germany during the rise of Hitler, and likely know it "didn't do enough" and somehow failed to stand. But exactly what didn't they do that they might have done? And what did they do that they shouldn't have done? Of course, our judging the German Church of that time implies that we believe we would not have made the mistakes they did—and yet we are making those same mistakes now.

Perhaps because of the unprecedented size of the tragedies and horrors of that era, it is particularly tempting for us to put them in a separate category from anything that could happen anywhere else.

---

[1] Eric Metaxas, *Bonhoeffer: Pastor, Martyr, Prophet, Spy* (Nashville, TN: Thomas Nelson, 2010).

Many of us have unwittingly adopted a tribalist and racist view of the Germans of that era, and attribute to them a unique level of evil, as though it has no bearing on us, nor can it ever have any bearing on us. But if we are Christians who believe in the doctrine of Original Sin, we know that our own intrinsic evil is perfectly equal to whatever we wish to attribute to the souls living in Germany in the 1930s. Therefore, we need to be more honest and ask how it was that they failed so spectacularly, knowing that we too can fail similarly—and are indeed this minute failing precisely as they failed.

So before we continue, we must dispense with the idea that we are for some reason incapable of allowing things to get to the point that the German Church did. That's precisely why I am writing this book: Because what I see happening in the American Church today makes me understand that we are wrong to think we would have acted differently if we were alive then precisely because we are not acting differently now.

As we approach the story of the German Church's failures, we should do so not only with some humility, but with some humiliation. That's because they did not have the benefit that we have—of actually seeing what happens when a church fails to stand. They did not have the example of what happened to them because it had not yet happened. But we do have that example and that grimmest of warnings, and so we are without excuse.

So what exactly did the German Church of that time fail to see? In a word: the future.

Christians are expected to see the future, or to listen to those who see it. We know that God is outside time; for Him the past, present, and future are equally easy to see. And we know that He has spoken through prophets who can, and often do, tell us what lies ahead, if we are interested in hearing it. So the real question is never whether we can see the future but whether we heed the warnings of the prophets who do. As we shall see, Dietrich Bonhoeffer was a prophet to the German Church in the 1930s, although he wouldn't have thought of himself in quite that way. But he spoke boldly and powerfully about where things stood in the German Church and about what must be done, and we know that the German Church did not take his warnings seriously and paid the gravest price imaginable.

But what if Bonhoeffer is a prophet to us today? Will the words that fell on deaf ears in his day fall differently on ours? Will we hear what he has to say, or rather, what God has to say through him? Since we have the dramatic advantage of knowing what happened in Germany, will we take what he said to them more seriously than they did? Will you?

✷

Part of what the German Church failed to see in 1932 or 1933, for example—when there was still time to act—was that their small actions or inactions were setting the course for their future. When God speaks through prophets like Bonhoeffer, He makes clear what lies ahead and gives us a clear choice. If we do X, Y will result, and if we don't, then Z. But many German church leaders thought Bonhoeffer a bit of a young hothead—a brilliant intellectual to be sure, but one who was overstating what was at stake. And so, as people always do—and always with good intentions—most of the German Church simply ignored what he said and drifted along as it had always done. They didn't feel the urgency that Bonhoeffer obviously felt and boldly spoke about. When they might have recognized where their actions were leading and changed course, they did not. It takes courage to stand athwart history and shout, "Stop!" It takes courage to understand that you must not do what everyone else is doing. Most of us rarely rise to such courage. But why and exactly how did the German Church ignore Bonhoeffer's prophetic warnings?

To tell this story we must begin at the end of 1932, two months before Hitler became chancellor, when Bonhoeffer gave a certain sermon in a certain church in Berlin.

Chapter Three

"Unless You Repent"

*"But I have this against you, that you have abandoned the love
you had at first. Remember therefore from where you have fallen;
repent, and do the works you did at first. If not, I will come to
you and remove your lampstand from its place,
unless you repent."*

—*REVELATION* 2:4–5

On November 6, 1932—Reformation Sunday—Bonhoeffer gave a sermon we may, with the benefit of hindsight, reckon as "prophetic." The church in which he gave it was the Kaiser-Wilhelm-*Gedächtniskirche*. In English it is called the Kaiser Wilhelm Memorial Church—and it was very much one of those churches—a place where anyone who was anyone in certain circles of Berlin society would wish to be seen, where one could burnish one's social bona fides and be thought of as part of the elite "in" crowd of that time and place.

We have very few churches like that in the United States today, where one's attendance might add to one's social standing. There are perhaps some in places like Dallas or Houston. But in its most elite circles, our culture has become so secular that it's a bit hard for us to relate to what that church was like to Berliners at that time. We might conceivably think of Episcopal churches along the lines of the National Cathedral in Washington, D.C.—or St. Patrick's Cathedral on Fifth Avenue in Manhattan, or perhaps St. Thomas's. In any event, where Bonhoeffer was invited to speak that Sunday was at the apex of such churches in Germany. Indeed, it was the very church to which that great national treasure Paul von Hindenburg would go whenever he attended church.

At the time of Bonhoeffer's sermon in 1932, Hindenburg was the chancellor of Germany. But really, he was much more than this, being at that time as celebrated and famous a figure as the nation could boast. At age eighty-five, he was more like a stout waxworks image of his former self—almost a living statue. If we can imagine the popularity of someone like General George Patton at the end of World War II, we have some idea of the figure Hindenburg cut, but even that cannot do justice to how Germans regarded him at the time. In any case, this was the venerable church he would occasionally grace with his impossibly august presence. Certainly, we should cringe to think of a human being gracing a church with his presence; after all, it is only God who graces a church with His presence. But sometimes we fallen human beings lose sight of these things, and this was the sort of church in which one was strongly tempted to do so.

The magnificent edifice was built in the 1890s by Kaiser Wilhelm II, who named it for his grandfather, Kaiser Wilhelm I, principally to show government support for—and solidarity with—the German Church. Of course, this was long before anyone in Germany dreamt that an anti-Christian maniac like Adolf Hitler would rule the country, so there was no fear of blurring the line between church and state. On the contrary, blurring that line was the point.

In the view of Kaiser Wilhelm II and many others, the twin authorities of church and state must stand together, and the interior of the church that bore his grandfather's name was calculated to make this point. It was decorated with huge, gorgeous, and exquisitely rendered mosaic murals portraying the kaiser and his queen in full imperial regalia of bejeweled crowns, medals, ermine, and sable. Just above these boldly colored mosaics were smaller and less resplendent images of Jesus and other biblical figures. This particular conflation of church and state will—and rightly should—make most American Christians uncomfortable. But this is mainly because we have a long history in our country of the separation of church and state. It is something we have valued from our founding nearly two and a half centuries ago. We cannot imagine huge portraits of Washington and Lincoln in our churches.

But we also cringe at the thought of this in that particular church in Germany because we now know—from the example of what took place under Hitler—that if the lines between church and state are not kept bright and clear, religious liberty can be thrown out the window and an all-powerful state can crush the Church under its heel and out of existence. That is precisely what the American Founders feared, and it is why they made the separation of church and state so central: they knew that in time, the state would be tempted to control the Church and would effectively wipe it out. As we have said, however, the church in which Bonhoeffer preached that day was built decades before anything of the kind would rear its ugly death's head in Germany. The dangers that might arise from a strong link between church and state were hardly considered, if at all.

Nonetheless, when Bonhoeffer was invited to speak there, he was himself considering that issue, for he was far more sensitive to the situation than most. There was little doubt in any circles that the golden epoch of Germany under the kaisers was already light-years in the past. That world had ended once and for all in 1918, when Germany was devastated by its loss in the First World War, and the Allied powers had forced the kaiser to abdicate. To many, it must have seemed as though a heavy iron portcullis had come crashing down, forever barring entry to that former world. The German nation had been wandering outside the camp ever since. But this didn't keep most people from wishing they might return to those days somehow, or perhaps from deluding themselves that they had never really left them and that all could go on as before.

Dietrich Bonhoeffer, however, was not deluded along such lines. On the contrary, he saw the real state of the German Church, and it horrified him. As a devoted Lutheran Christian, he knew that the fiery church of Luther—whose legacy they were celebrating that very day—had long since disappeared. It had been replaced by pro forma "religion." It was Christianity without Christ. Around this time, he began thinking deeply about this subject, and would eventually put his thoughts in his famous book, *The Cost of Discipleship*, published in 1937.

So that day Bonhoeffer doubtless saw what was being celebrated in that church as concerning. He knew that when the German Lutheran church had become so comfortable that it ceased to see what it really means to follow Christ, danger was at hand. By that time, Germany and Lutheranism—which is to say church and state—had effectively melted together in many people's minds. And on this Reformation Day when everyone celebrated German Lutheranism, this reality was greatly underscored, at least for Bonhoeffer.

Bonhoeffer understood that if everyone who loved Germany was automatically thought of as a Lutheran Christian—almost as a birthright—then the heart of the Christian faith had become meaningless. This was what he saw on display in that Reformation Day celebration. It all seemed calculated to celebrate Luther and his legacy, and their Lutheran faith, and so it made a mockery both of Luther's profound devotion to Christ and to the otherworldly devotion that true faith in Christ demands of us.

Bonhoeffer was presciently and prophetically aware that at that moment in Germany, the tribalist pagan forces that put German pride ahead of God were in the ascendant, and on that day of all days, he knew he must speak out about it. He was hardly against patriotism, but he saw clearly that as Germany moved toward National Socialism, the nation was at a precipice. He knew he must help the people to see that, and only then might they repent, turn from that precipice, and save themselves from going over. They must see that Hitler's brand of German nationalism was a wicked perversion of healthy nationalism. It was the kind of nationalism that was the sworn enemy of Christianity and of Christ—and if they did not see that, the results would be catastrophic.

So that day Bonhoeffer delivered a sermon that many in the pews likely thought a jeremiad. It was certainly a philippic. Rather than stroke the egos of those German elites slumbering in the pews, Bonhoeffer's sermon was calculated to wake them up, if they were still able to be awakened. If it wasn't too late.

He was only twenty-six but already renowned as a theological genius, and he told them that day what almost no one else would have dared: their unbridled nationalistic celebration of Luther was a gruesome mistake. The German Church had strayed so far from the heroic church of Luther—who had risked his life for his faith—that Bonhoeffer was offended to see this carnal and ignorant exuberance. To him it seemed extraordinary that those celebrating "Reformation Day" would think that business as usual was acceptable.

In 1932 there were ideological currents swirling all around that would grow stronger if they weren't checked. Bonhoeffer knew that only a real Church in Germany could stand against them—and the Church was asleep. He saw the handwriting on the wall, and that day he wished to make his listeners see it too. If the German Church did not stop fooling around with these self-congratulatory exhibitions masquerading as church services—if it did not shake itself awake and begin seeing what was happening, and forcefully speak out against it—it would be swept away. If the Church did not arise as the true Church of Jesus Christ, but only continued to play at having church, tragedy was looming.

Would God not judge the German Church just as He had judged the people of Israel when they had forgotten Him? Bonhoeffer knew from Scripture that if the people of God did not act like the people of God, God sent His prophets; but if the prophets' warnings went unheeded, judgment fell. And so the young preacher did that day what the prophets had done in Israel millennia before: he warned God's people of what he saw, hoping they might see it, too, and repent before it was too late.

Two years earlier Bonhoeffer had spent nine months in the United States. Most of that time he was in New York, spending the 1930–31 academic year at Union Theological Seminary. That time seems to have played a huge role in his awakening to the issue of what it really meant to be a Christian. During his year in America, the Nazis had vaulted from obscurity to great prominence in the German Reichstag, which is that nation's parliament. Bonhoeffer knew the German Church was not in shape to stand against the powerful pagan and tribalistic forces being unleashed in his country. At the time of his sermon, Hitler was less than three months from becoming chancellor of the nation. It was an outcome desperately to be avoided, but Bonhoeffer could feel the inexorable drift in that direction. So that day he thundered like an Old Testament prophet, declaring to the horrified parishioners that the church of Martin Luther was dying—if not already dead. For any of them to pretend otherwise was nothing but a ghastly farce. In case anyone wondered whether this young man was serious, they could read the biblical text he had chosen that morning. The full text was from Revelation 2:4–5:

> But I have this against you, that you have abandoned the
> love you had at first. Remember therefore from where you
> have fallen; repent, and do the works you did at first. If not,

I will come to you and remove your lampstand from its place, unless you repent.

These were the chilling words of Jesus to the church in Ephesus. He was warning His people—just as He had done with the Israelites in the Old Testament—that if they did not heed His warning, terrible judgments would fall. Jesus was certainly not the nonjudgmental caricature that so many have made Him out to be. And in Revelation He appears to John as the fearsome Judge, so that when He speaks, we had better hear Him and take His warning with the deepest seriousness.

Bonhoeffer that day, in using that Scripture and in all that he said, was not pulling his punches. Unless the German Church saw where it stood and repented, God would judge it. Unless it stopped playing church as it was doing that day, and got serious about sincerely living out its faith, the results would be gruesome. But how could these comfortable people in that extraordinary setting hear what Bonhoeffer had to say? What was his evidence that the German Church was at the precipice he claimed? Was it not typical of young men to overstate things and to think that they must be at the forefront of dramatic developments in history? It was one thing for Jesus to speak that way to the church in Ephesus, but could they really take seriously the idea that He might speak to them that way? After all, theirs was a Christian nation, and had been for centuries.

In celebrating "Reformation Day," Luther, and Lutheranism, they were to some extent celebrating themselves. But Bonhoeffer in his sermon meant to get them to see the infinitely less flattering truth of the matter. "Protestantism is not about us and our protest against the world," he said, "but rather about God's protest against us: 'But I have this against you . . .'"

He made it personal, and it was not at all heartwarming or encouraging. He was saying that the German Church had drifted impossibly far from the church of Luther, and the Lord whose name they were mostly taking in vain had something against them, just as He had something against those in the church at Ephesus. Bonhoeffer valiantly warned his hearers that the same God who so chillingly warned the church in Ephesus also was speaking to them. They must hear the words of Jesus for themselves now: that if they did not see their error and repent, He would remove their "candlestick." The church in Ephesus had been specially marked by God, just as the German Church had been specially marked in its own way. But God had warned the Ephesians that if they continued on their path, he would remove the blessing and protection He had given them. And so too, Bonhoeffer made clear, would God judge the German Church if they did not hear what He was saying to them that day.

Bonhoeffer went on:

> But we are still pretending, aren't we? When it comes down to it, we know very well that it is not about "A mighty fortress," nor about "Here I stand"; this is not the protest we are talking about. We know full well about God's protest against us, and we know that, most of all on Reformation Day, God is out in force against us.
>
> But we don't want to admit it, either to ourselves or to the world. We are afraid we would look foolish in the eyes of God and the world if we admitted any such thing. That's why we make so much noise about this day, October 31, hammering wrong ideas into the hands of thousands of schoolchildren, only so that they don't notice our weakness, so that we can forget it ourselves.

No, our time has run out for such solemn church feast days on which we put on an act for ourselves. Let us stop celebrating the Reformation that way! Let us lay the dead Luther to rest at long last, and instead listen to the gospel, reading his Bible, hearing God's own word in it. At the last judgment God is certainly going to ask us not, "Have you celebrated Reformation Day properly?" but rather, "Have you heard my word and kept it?"[1]

There is much more to his sermon, and some of it is harsher than these few sentences. But as we might have guessed, it did not have anything close to the young preacher's intended effect. The congregation left their pews and continued behaving as they always had. They did not repent. Martin Luther—the man whose legacy they had so thoughtlessly come to celebrate—had stood against the arrayed powers of his day for what he believed, and had faced the extremely real threat of being burned alive for his "heresy." He was hounded and harassed, but his faith—lived out in his words and his actions—inspired others to follow him, and often even to die for what they believed.

But the German Church of Bonhoeffer's time had drifted far from this kind of faith, as if perhaps God wasn't paying very close attention anymore. Luther had feared the eternal flames of Hell more than he feared the flames he was being threatened with by those who condemned him, and he acted and spoke boldly. But what did the Lutheran church of Bonhoeffer's day fear? Losing their respectable positions in society? Did they fear anything at all?

We will discuss what followed in Germany in the years after this day in 1932. But since we are still at the scene of Bonhoeffer's sermon,

---

[1] Victoria J. Barnett, ed., *The Collected Sermons of Dietrich Bonhoeffer*, vol. 2 (Minneapolis, MN: Fortress Press, 2017), 95.

we may cut to the chase of this particular story and tell the reader exactly what happened to this particular church. Because what remains today of that once-glorious building is perhaps as dramatic a picture of divine judgment as we are likely to get in modern times.

The destruction of the Kaiser Wilhelm Memorial Church did not come about by lightning bolt, but by the English bombs dropped by the RAF in November 1943. In the larger effort to shatter Hitler's capital city, and with it, the already-foundering Nazi war machine, they nearly obliterated this historic building. In the nearly eleven years since Bonhoeffer's sermon, Germany's indifference to what he said had matured to its full fruition. By the time of the church's destruction, the whole world was at war. Millions had already died and millions more would follow. And most horribly, millions more were being systematically murdered in the death camps that had bloomed since Germany's officials gathered in January 1942 at Wannsee, where they had solved "The Jewish Question" by vowing to direct many of their dwindling national resources away from winning the war against the Allies, and toward killing as many innocent Jews as possible. It is certainly the most macabre solution to any "question" in human history. We rarely have as clear a picture of God's warning followed by His judgment, unless of course one cannot bring oneself to see any direct connection. Such things are almost always easier to wave away as coincidental. We hardly want to believe that God judges in that way anymore.

But if you visit Berlin, you owe it to yourself to see with your own eyes what remains of the once-magnificent church. After the bombings it might still conceivably have been repaired. But the mood after the war was to let the ghastly ruin stand as a heavy-handed reminder of the horrors of war, as though that were necessary. A hideous modernist building was affixed to it which now functions as the church there, unintentionally underscoring the abject awfulness of it all.

But one can still walk into the bombed center of the old building under the cracked and pitted bell tower and see the mosaic murals of the old kaiser and his queen. And while one stands there, it becomes difficult not to wonder how Bonhoeffer's prophetic warning in that very spot went unheeded, and indeed came true in such a dramatic and graphic way.

While we are at it, we might further wonder whether the shattered visage of that once-magnificent building may help us take God's warnings to us more seriously, and encourage us in the American Church to heed His message—through Bonhoeffer—for ourselves.

Chapter Four

"The Church and the Jewish Question"

Three months after Bonhoeffer's sermon—on January 31, 1933—Adolf Hitler came to power as the chancellor of the German nation. Though he was wisely coy about the details, he was nonetheless deeply dedicated to fundamentally changing Germany. This meant bringing everything in German life, including the German Church, into line with Nazi doctrines. Once he had the power and the opportunity to act, Hitler did so with lightning speed, and things changed very quickly. Some of the changes were official, in the form of legislation and decrees, as we shall see, but others were less obvious.

For example, just two days after Hitler came to power, Bonhoeffer gave an important radio address. It had been scheduled for some time, so he did not give it as a response to Hitler's ascension. But in that address, given on the first day of February 1933, Bonhoeffer spoke pointedly on "Leadership," and specifically on something called "The Leadership Principle" ("*Führerprinzip*"), an idea that had been popular in Germany over the previous two decades and which was centrally important to Hitler's view of himself.

The German word for "leader" is "Führer," and Hitler had, with evil brilliance, put himself forward as *the* Leader—*Der Führer*—that Germany needed at that time. He presented himself as the living embodiment of this idea, and there can be no question that it had messianic overtones to anyone paying attention, as Bonhoeffer certainly was. So when Bonhoeffer addressed the question of "Leadership" in his speech, he was trying to explain that the biblical idea of leadership was dramatically and utterly opposed to Hitler's idea of it. The Bible speaks of servant leadership: "He who would be first must be last." Jesus Himself famously modeled this idea for His disciples on Maundy Thursday, when He took on the role of a lowly slave and washed their feet. Bonhoeffer contended in his address that if a leader's main objective was to idolize himself, that leader was not exhibiting true, godly leadership, but was in fact a "mis-leader" of the people he pretended to lead.

We in America have always understood the biblical idea of leadership, whether we explicitly recognized it as such or didn't. If "we the people" are to govern ourselves, we are obliged to reject the idea of leaders who do not serve those whom they lead. Though we have sometimes forgotten about it, our American idea of self-government comes to us in no small part from the biblical model, in which the Israelites made a covenant directly with God. So we can easily see how the popular Führer Principle that catapulted Hitler to power and helped him stay there would have been deeply distasteful to someone like Bonhoeffer.

It was a bold and vital speech that Bonhoeffer gave that day on the subject. But because Hitler was now chancellor, something strange happened. Somewhere in the middle of the speech, the broadcast was cut off. No one knew for sure whether higher-ups in the Nazi regime made this happen, but it is hard to imagine that they hadn't. Circumstances in Germany had changed quite suddenly, and what would have gone swimmingly a week earlier might no longer work at all. To put it in our own modern parlance, Bonhoeffer had just been "cancelled." There were many similar experiences to come for him, but this was his own first taste of the new world into which all Germans had just entered.

One of the important themes of Bonhoeffer's life story—and of this book too—is that we must change along with our circumstances. The evil of today is different than the evil of yesterday or of tomorrow, and when Jesus enjoins us to be "shrewd as serpents," it means we must understand this. We must not be thoughtlessly sucked along into the mainstream of popular thinking, since that is often the broad road that leads to destruction. We have to take care to read the signs of the times. And no one understood this and lived it out better than Dietrich Bonhoeffer.

He understood that with Hitler now officially in charge, Germans who opposed him would have to be cannier. But as Bonhoeffer tried to wake up the German Church leaders, he was constantly battling with people who simply could not see the changing situation, or accept that it was changing—and that it required them to change their approach. They seemed to think that what might have worked in 1915 or 1925 would work in 1935. They were not alive to the urgency of the situation. These were the same people who were convinced they could continue as they had always done, who believed that would suffice, that that was the path forward. They refused to see the new situation and to act accordingly.

We will go into the roughly four reasons for this in the chapters following, but the fact is that because of their inability to see things clearly, they clung to what was safe; and in doing so they markedly departed from leaning on God and trusting Him with what lay ahead. They had become so comfortable with "business as usual" that they had entirely forgotten how to lean on God—and so, when things changed and it was dramatically required that they do so, they did not.

As we have touched on already, a very similar dynamic is at work in the American Church today. Many pastors and leaders sincerely believe that we can—and should—continue as we have been doing for decades. We should "preach the Gospel" and "teach the Bible" as we always have done, and we must act as though the current state of our culture and nation is essentially the same as it has always been. But most people in the pews whom these pastors purport to lead know that things are not as they were even a few years ago. They are looking to their pastoral leaders to acknowledge this, to help them understand what is happening and to lead them in standing against it.

After all, isn't this precisely why they have been studying the Bible and listening to sermons over the years? Was not all of that preparation for this hour? But in most churches, the business as usual continues. As though they might kick the current troubles away, the leaders simply continue preparing for something in the future, which they seem to hope will simply never come. Many Christians are abandoning such churches for the few that are alive to the situation, where the pastors are less timid about saying what needs to be said. But in the increasing numbers of those churches that refuse to see where we are and address it, has God not already begun to bring about His judgment? Has he not already cursed the fig tree?

✚

But to better understand where we are, we return to the German Church at the beginning of the Nazi regime. As soon as Hitler came to power, he swiftly began to make his moves toward subduing it. He knew the amicable history between the German Church and state would make it unlikely that many would see what he was up to. Of course, he did not speak openly about what he had in mind, because if anyone was "shrewd as a serpent" it was Adolf Hitler. But Bonhoeffer saw precisely what was happening and began to speak out about it to the German Church leadership. He saw clearly that a reckoning was on the horizon. It was not possible for the Church to remain the Church if it submitted to Nazi leadership. Biblical thinking and Nazi ideology deviated dramatically on fundamental points. But most German Christian leaders simply did not see this when Hitler first took power. They did not connect the dots.

But Bonhoeffer did. It is extraordinary how quickly the Nazis moved to change things—and how quickly they acted to destroy the democratic processes that had been in place for so long. But it is perhaps even more extraordinary to see how quickly Bonhoeffer recognized what was happening and responded to it.

What the Nazis did first, a mere four weeks into Hitler's chancellorship, was to use the incident of the Reichstag Fire—in which a Dutch madman set fire to the German Parliament building—to enact sweeping emergency decrees that suddenly allowed Hitler to do things without the approval of the German Parliament. It was a stunning erasure of German government, with blitzkrieg swiftness. It is still a question whether the Nazis themselves enabled the arson so they could use it as a pretext for what they did next. The Nazis controlled the media narrative and instantly whipped up a hysterical fear of the "Communists" and their other political opponents, whom they insisted were to blame for the burning of the Reichstag despite evidence to the contrary. But it was a useful fiction, and in order to do the things they wished to do, they needed to demonize their enemies—many of whom were rounded up and imprisoned—and to crush dissent by instilling fear in anyone who wished to object. Can you think of parallels to our own time?

The Reichstag Fire paved the way for much else. Soon thereafter—on April 7, 1933—Hitler signed the "Restoration Act." In the Nazis' efforts to create a racially "pure" German state, they had included the so-called "Aryan Paragraph" in this law, which suddenly made it illegal for anyone with Jewish blood to hold a government position. In time, these antisemitic restrictions would be extended to other professions, as the Nazis were always expanding their powers over German society. But it was the "Aryan Paragraph" that clarified things rather dramatically for the German Church and brought things to a head, because the German Lutheran Church was officially part of the German government. Could the German Church suddenly change its doctrines to submit to the Nazis' racial ideology?

As almost everyone knows, in the Christian church, anyone who adheres to its beliefs is welcome. So if in Germany a pastor happened to have Jewish blood—as many did—this was perfectly immaterial. In fact, Bonhoeffer's closest friend at that time, Franz Hildebrandt, was ethnically Jewish. He had come to believe in the doctrines of the Christian Church and to be baptized and, like Bonhoeffer, was ordained as a pastor. If the Aryan Paragraph was accepted by the German Church, as the Nazis insisted, Hildebrandt and any other ethnically Jewish pastors would be legally barred from serving.

Naturally this was unacceptable to Bonhoeffer. How could the German state dare tell the Church of Jesus Christ who its members and leaders could be? The Church always had the freedom to determine this. The biblical view is that God looks on our hearts and doesn't care whether someone who believes in Jesus is a Jew or a non-Jew. And of course, Jesus was Himself a Jew, as were each of the twelve disciples and most in the early Church. That the Nazi government would suddenly wipe away two millennia with one stroke and determine that the German Church must be organized along racial and antisemitic lines was perfect madness and obviously untenable.

But what's amazing and horrifying is that many in the German Church—like many in the American Church now—were willing to look the other way, even on something that touched the very fundamentals of the faith in which they professed to believe. They wished to get along and not to be seen as "troublemakers." But Bonhoeffer was not among them, nor were those in what was then called the "Emergency Pastors League," a group of heroic pastors who saw what was happening and turned to Bonhoeffer to think through and put in writing what he believed were the Church's obligations under the dramatically changing circumstances.

In April 1933 Bonhoeffer wrote his essay, "The Church and the Jewish Question," in which he spells out rather clearly what he saw as the German Church's role in dealing with the circumstances arising from a state hostile to Christian belief. If anyone doubts whether Bonhoeffer believed Christians could get "political," they need only read this document, which may be summed up by its three central points.

First, Bonhoeffer said the Church was the conscience of the state and must call it to account, that it must loudly object if the state was doing wrong. It could not—and must not—remain silent when injustices and wrongs were being promoted and enacted. Second, he said that the Christian Church was obligated to help any victims of the state. For Bonhoeffer, that clearly included the Jews. But thirdly, and most dramatically, Bonhoeffer concluded that if the state refused to change course and do the right thing, but rather continued in its sins—which in this case were principally focused on persecuting the Jews—it was the solemn obligation of Christians to take action. They were not merely to protest verbally and to help the victims, but were also to become actively political—to "shove a stick in the spokes" of the wheel of the rumbling machine of the state.

To some pastors who heard Bonhoeffer deliver this essay, it was all rather shocking. Some even walked out. But already in early 1933

Bonhoeffer saw—and said—that those who call themselves Christians have an obligation to God to get "political" if necessary, and to take a bold—and likely dangerous—stand against their own government. This was a markedly radical departure from the default mode of the German churches since the time of Luther, whose memorable embracing of Romans 13 constituted a kind of *Summum Bonum* on the subject, as though it was all that needed to be said about the relations between church and state, as we shall explain.

Chapter Five

12,000 Pastors

As it happened, what Bonhoeffer so clearly said in "The Church and the Jewish Question" was not at all clear to most pastors in Germany. They balked at its conclusions, which seemed to them premature and radical. Even many of those whom Bonhoeffer knew to be his allies in this fight thought he was being unmeasured and hasty in pushing them to take a united and dramatic stand against the Nazis. Surely the Nazis might be reasoned with. Surely things would shape themselves in a more positive direction over time. It would never do for august pastors and ministers to seem unreasonable, or nakedly political, or—God forbid—political enemies of the state.

This was tremendously frustrating for Bonhoeffer, because he knew that unless the German Church leaders clearly saw the urgency of what was happening and acted with even greater urgency, all would be lost. As long as they dithered and debated, the Nazis would retain the upper hand, and would win. Did these pastors not understand that things had changed dramatically and that they must respond dramatically? With each day that passed, the deeply unscrupulous

Nazis masterfully exploited the scrupulousness—or actually the overscrupulousness—of the timid pastors, and thereby consolidated more power. The clock was ticking, and Bonhoeffer saw that if the German Church was not decisive and heroic in that hour, it would soon lack even the ability to fight back. It would be taken away from them. Indeed, it was being taken away from them with every minute that passed. The window was closing on whatever chances they had.

Did they not understand that actually being a follower of Jesus entailed radical obedience? Did they not remember that Luther had faced death and that many who had followed him had faced death—and that many were put to death? Did they think their Lutheran Christian faith was somehow exempt from such things? What had become of their faith so that it was now so flabby and unable to stand against the enemies of God in their time?

✣

As 1933 wore on, the main battle lines in the German Church itself were shown to lie between the devotedly pro-Nazi *Deutsche Christen*, who zealously wished to help Hitler form and oversee a national Reich Church on the one side, and those in what came to be called the *Bekennende Kirche* (the "Confessing Church") on the other.

It is always the temptation of a powerful state to push the Church around, but in Germany this was not an issue until the Nazis seized control. As we have said, in previous years and most recently under the kaisers, the German Church was comfortably aligned with the German state. But suddenly the leader of the state was Adolf Hitler, who privately despised the Church and Christianity generally, though he certainly wouldn't say so openly. He worked very cannily in giving the German Church the idea that he was with them, all the while working to co-opt and undermine them. Those in his inner circle knew precisely what he thought of the Church and its despicable "Jewish" theology, and they knew he had inordinate ambitions to bring it to heel under his own leadership. But it had to be done carefully.

Bonhoeffer—along with such other figures as Martin Niemöller and Karl Barth—knew they must draw a line in the sand. If the Nazis succeeded in creating a "Reich Church" subservient to Hitler, the Church in Germany would effectively be dead. We should say that whenever a church is subservient to the state or to the reigning worldly culture—as the official church in communist China is today—it is no longer the Church of Jesus Christ. It is a counterfeit church that does not serve Jesus, but that serves the forces of power, which is to say it serves the devil.

Before the Nazis could murder the actual Christian Church, the aforementioned Christian leaders in 1934 drafted and published what has come to be called the Barmen Declaration. It essentially said that the German state must not and could not co-opt the Church, that the sanctity and separation of the Church from the state must be clear. All who signed this document were known as the *Bekennende Kirche*—or "Confessing Church"—and they declared it to be the true church in Germany, free from Nazi interference and submitted only to God.

But what is shocking to us today is that most pastors in Germany were not willing to sign it. Either they were not thinking clearly on the subject at hand, and as a result were not thinking biblically, or perhaps they were thinking clearly enough, but they simply did not have the courage to act on what they knew to be true. Perhaps they—like so many in the American Church today—thought it safer to sit on the sidelines and do nothing, to see which way the wind was blowing, so to speak.

It is worth noting that the great Charles Colson saw troubling signs here in America and, taking a page from the Barmen Declaration—along with Princeton's Robert P. George and Beeson Divinity School's Timothy George—drafted what came to be called "The Manhattan Declaration" in 2009. It saw on the horizon what the American Church is now facing and wished to get Christians and Christian leaders to sign it, so that we might all—Catholic, Protestant, and Orthodox—be on the record as standing firmly for biblical principles with regard to the state.

For example, the state could not force medical professionals to perform abortions, or to do anything that might violate their religious liberty. The state could not force anyone to violate their biblical views regarding marriage between a man and a woman. And if the state did attempt to force Christians to violate their consciences, we were obligated to be civilly disobedient. The document cited Martin Luther King Jr.'s "Letter from Birmingham Jail" to this end.

But just as with the Barmen Declaration, many high-profile pastors—many of whom were Colson's friends—nonetheless demurred in signing it. Just as so many otherwise faithful pastors in Germany had done in the 1930s, they grasped at various theological straws to exempt themselves, and at many of precisely the same straws too.

When Colson the following year read my newly published biography of Bonhoeffer, his feelings toward these pastors and friends at repeating these grave errors erupted in annotations in the book's margins, where he even named some of them: "Begg, Piper, and MacArthur."[1] How could these dear brothers, of all people, be so theologically fussy that they did not see what was at stake?

✠

We know that the unwillingness of so many in Germany to understand what was happening and to act decisively was fatal. In 1935, a

[1] After Chuck's death, his widow Patty gave me his copy of my book.

year after the Barmen Declaration was drafted, there were roughly eighteen thousand Protestant pastors in Germany. We aren't sure exactly how many of them actually signed the Barmen Declaration and identified themselves with the Confessing Church. It seems to have been nearly six thousand. But what we do know is that the Nazis were so aggressive in persecuting those who dared to stand against them that already by 1935, only about three thousand of the eighteen thousand pastors stood strongly on the side of the Confessing Church. It is sobering that only one-sixth of German pastors dared to stand on what we can now see as an extremely important principle. But the facts are what they are, and they stand as a grave warning to us today. Are we under the illusion that we are somehow different than they?

Roughly the same number—three thousand—were part of the *Deutsche Kristen*, who staunchly stood with Hitler *against* the Confessing Church. But perhaps most interesting in this portrait of the Protestant Church in Germany of that time are the twelve thousand who weren't willing to take a stand one way or the other. One presumes most of them agreed with the Confessing Church, but somehow they simply didn't have the courage to take a bold stand along such lines. It seems they reckoned it the better part of valor to let the three thousand take all the heat. The twelve thousand preferred to remain "neutral," as if this were possible.

But can we doubt that it is precisely because of the twelve thousand who did not stand strongly with the Confessing Church that the three thousand who did had a much harder time? If another three thousand or six thousand Protestant pastors had stood with the Confessing Church during this time, the Nazis could never have been able to succeed, which is an extraordinary and heartbreaking thing to consider. But the church had great cultural power in Germany. So when it balked and chose not to use its voice and its cultural power, it doomed the entirety of the German Church, which in turn doomed the whole nation. The blood of the scores of millions who died in the Second World War and the blood of the millions murdered in that abomination we call the Holocaust is on the hands of those twelve thousand. And when innocent blood cries out to God for justice, God, who is a Judge, judges. God certainly judged Germany and the German Church, most of whose leaders were sure He would not. Will God judge the American Church? Do we, like the Germans, think we are somehow exempt? Is there still time for us to repent, or is it already too late?

Before we continue, a word to those who do not believe we have time to repent, who believe that God must judge us because of what we already have done—and not done. Such beliefs are not biblical, and those who hold them are themselves enjoined to repent. To sulk like Jonah at what seems to be God's forbearance with those we deem irredeemably wicked is only to become the enemies of God ourselves. Those who petulantly have decided that nothing we do now can avert judgment are themselves participating in bringing about that judgment by doing nothing. Their unwillingness to fight now will likely be the very thing that makes the crucial difference. It is ironic and tragic that they sit on the sidelines alongside those they blame for the situation.

The latter sit there doing nothing because they think all will be well—that God has evolved into a kinder, gentler soul than the primitive deity who judged ancient Israel and dared to threaten the removal of the Ephesian church's candlestick, and who may conceivably, as lately as the last century, have judged Germany. The former group sits on the sidelines and also does nothing, but as this second group sits, they lift their eyes to the heavens and rub their hands with glee at God's imminent judgment, earnestly desiring to see the Almighty hurry up and do what they have decided He must do—even if He hasn't yet done it, and even if their sitting on the sidelines is part of the reason for His having to do it eventually.

✳

We know what followed in Germany. Because the twelve thousand pastors chose not to be "political" and shrank from taking a heroic stand, the Nazis were successfully able to marginalize—and then openly demonize—the three thousand who strongly stood with the Confessing Church. With the silence and compliance of the twelve thousand, they began arresting and otherwise persecuting those pastors who had been willing to take a stand. In 1935 alone, the Nazis arrested seven hundred such pastors.

One wonders what the twelve thousand were thinking as they witnessed these things. Of course, some of them realized they had been wrong in hanging back, but perhaps now it was too late, and they would have to live with their regrets for the rest of their lives, as so many did. But others likely were affirmed in their inactions when they saw what the Nazis did to those who had so boldly opposed them. They felt that they had been wise to stay out of trouble, and perhaps thought that those hotheads being persecuted only deserved what they got.

But what is certain to us today, who can see what happened, is that almost no one dreamt how far things would go. No one seemed to see that by submitting to the tremendous cultural pressure to conform to the Nazi way of thinking in the beginning they were aiding and abetting it. Of course, things would not resolve themselves amicably, as they fondly and naïvely hoped, but would rage on like a swollen river that would o'erleap its banks and cause such destruction so far and wide as no one ever could have possibly imagined. Surely many of those twelve thousand—if they early on had gotten a glimpse of the future and seen the millions of emaciated corpses of innocent men, women, and children in the death camps—would have behaved differently.

Once again, we must put ourselves in their shoes, because the mistakes they made are precisely the mistakes many in the American Church are making today. The Germans didn't think such evil things could happen, and of course we now know they were wrong. But let's be honest: the tremendous evilness of evil is difficult to take in. Sometimes, however, God requires us to take it in—and to stand against it. But the German Christians of that time could not bring themselves to face it and always imagined things were not as bad as they were hearing from the likes of Bonhoeffer.

They could not believe that the Nazis were devotedly anti-Christian—and that they were essentially atheist and pagan tribalists working to eventually obliterate the Christian Church. In mostly willful ignorance of these things, they blithely went along with the general mood of the time, feeling that was the safest course. Many churches hung Nazi banners and flags outside their churches, and even inside their sanctuaries. It was a small but significant departure from the idea of displaying the German flag, which any German Church happily would have done before this time. But healthy patriotism was no longer enough, so hanging the swastika—what was called the "Crooked Cross"—may be seen as the virtue-signaling of that time. It may also be plausibly compared to when well-meaning churches today display rainbow banners or BLM flags. Most of them "know not what they do" and are only trying to show solidarity with those they have deemed somehow disenfranchised. They only wish to show that they are not like those other rigid and narrow-minded churches, that they are inclusive, and generally mean no harm. They don't seem to know that the forces behind those banners are only smiling at them in order to deceive them; as soon as they have the cultural and political power, they will show their dedicatedly atheist colors, and will show very clearly what they think of such quaint Christian virtues as mercy and humility and love of one's enemies. This is too painful for many to imagine, so they simply look away and denounce those who would point such things out. At present they are gaily riding on the back of a tiger, and all seems well enough.

Although many might be shocked to hear such comparisons, we must understand that our shock is only because we have the advantage of knowing what eventually happened in Germany. We must be clear that in the beginning of these troubles—in 1933 and 1934 especially—few Germans saw the swastika as anything but benign. They could not dream of what it would come to mean in the years ahead, that what seemed a hopeful symbol of the new Germany would one day strike fear into the hearts of millions, with downright satanic overtones. In these earliest years of the Nazi regime, most pastors only knew that if they went along with the crowd in showing support for the Führer they would be thought of as above suspicion and left alone. After all, were they not patriotic Germans too? They were simply making sure that others knew they were patriotic Germans, that they didn't wish to take any dramatic stand against the current regime. It was for many a way of publicly saying they were only interested in doing their job and staying within the confines of their own religious sphere. They only wished to "preach the Gospel" and not to take any "political" stand.

So to be fair to many of these twelve thousand pastors in these first years, the idea that Hitler would gain a death grip on the nation for twelve long years was unthinkable. And the idea that he would create death camps in which millions would be murdered was not even a cloud on the horizon the size of a man's fist. No one dreamt of it. Though it may seem inconceivable to us today, the Final Solution, in which Nazi leaders gathered at the infamous Wannsee conference to determine the grim fate of the Jews, did not take place until 1942, halfway into the Second World War. So the plan to exterminate untold millions of innocents—which we now automatically associate with the swastika—was virtually unimaginable when the Nazis first took power.

But Bonhoeffer could somehow see what lay ahead, and knew the concessions the Church was making would be fatal in the years to come. He knew that in their ignorance, silence, inaction, and theological confusion, they were not only helping evil gain a foothold, but were lending evil a helping hand.

Chapter Six

The Spiral of Silence

Silence in the face of evil is itself evil. Not to speak is to speak.
Not to act is to act. God will not hold us guiltless.

Although the familiar phrase above cannot be directly traced to Bonhoeffer, it has nonetheless become associated with him inasmuch as it so well sums up what he was desperately trying to communicate to those who believed they could safely stand on the sidelines in the battle of that time. Bonhoeffer knew that the time to stand on the sidelines had passed, and that if one was not actively living out one's faith by fighting against the wickedness of the Nazis, God would reckon that inaction as participation in their wicked cause with the added sin that those guilty of this were pretending to be neutral. God was not fooled.

Around the time of his involvement in the Manhattan Declaration, Chuck Colson referred to the concept called the "Spiral of Silence," which he had encountered in the work of German sociologist and political scientist Elisabeth Noelle-Neumann. She coined it in the 1970s when writing about what had happened in Germany in the 1930s. Born in Berlin in 1916, she had lived through the Nazi regime and was herself generally pro-Hitler, and had even met him while a university student. But when the war was over and everyone saw the inexpressible horrors of the Holocaust, she began to think differently. She wondered most specifically why so few of those who had privately opposed Hitler said nothing until the war was over and the danger of speaking out had passed. From this she came up with this concept called the "Spiral of Silence." It refers to the idea that when people fail to speak, the price of speaking rises. As the price to speak rises, still fewer speak out, which further causes the price to rise, so that fewer people yet will speak out, until a whole culture or nation is silenced. This was what happened in Germany.

So the idea attributed to Bonhoeffer, that "silence in the face of evil is itself evil," is borne out in Noelle-Neumann's formulation. If you do not speak, you are not being neutral, but are contributing to the success of the thing you refuse to name and condemn.

Contrarily, it follows that those who speak out make it easier for others to speak out. Just as cowardice begets cowardice, courage begets courage. When we speak out, we inevitably encourage others to speak out along with us, decreasing the price of speaking out. So there is no way to remain neutral in such situations. Either we help evil, or we fight evil. Either we speak and thereby help others to speak truth, or we cower in silence and thereby lead others to do the same.

Perhaps the main question for most of us is whether we are willing to pay the price of speaking and acting. If we truly understand the situation, as many of the twelve thousand pastors in Germany did, what do we fear in speaking out? Do pastors who fear speaking out really fear that they will lose congregants and that their tithes will decrease and their church will wither away, so that in their own minds they are simply being prudent? Do they know that God has called them to their position and that He grew their church and can be counted on to take care of them and their careers if they lean on Him and do what they believe He is calling them to do? What exactly keeps any of us from doing the right thing? We Christians claim to believe that Jesus defeated death on the cross—so if we say that we are sincere Christians but fear anything, including death, we are fools. Does not our fear of anything but God Himself make of God a liar?

Of course there are many things that contribute to our silence today and to the silence of those in the German Church of that era. It may not merely be a simple lack of real faith, or a simple lack of real courage. It is often a combination of several things, including some genuine theological objections and misunderstandings—which are worth identifying, if only to better understand how they came to exist and why they still hold power over many of us today. Because if we do not understand the roots of our fear and silence, and do not repent of these things in the shortest possible term, there is no question that we will end as the German Church ended after its own historical failures. God is no respecter of persons, and if we believe we are exempt from His judgments, we will learn the hard way that we are mistaken.

There are four principal ways in which our misunderstandings have helped us to the current unpleasant and momentous pass. The first of these errors has to do with our misunderstanding of the meaning of the word "faith," which we have cheapened and which is directly related to Bonhoeffer's idea of "cheap grace." The second error has to do with what we may call the "idol of evangelism." This is the unbiblical idea that the only real role the Church has is evangelism, so we must never say anything that might in any way detract from our pursuing this single goal. A third error may be summed up by the false commandment "Be Ye Not Political," which is a wrong-headed view of the Church's proper relationship to the state, leading to the idea that politics is off limits and beyond the boundary of our faith. Finally, and fourth in our list of errors, is the pietistic and perfectly negative idea that our Christian faith is lived out principally by avoiding sin, so that we must place our own virtue and salvation above all other matters. Like the ideas that evangelism is everything and that we may not be political, this idea is perfectly paralyzing and prevents the believer from living and acting freely under God's grace. Each of these errors is somehow connected to the others, but for the purposes of clarity, we will deal with them in turn, one at a time.

Chapter Seven

Two Errors of Faith

Theological and other errors often arise in reaction to a previous error. In other words, by reacting so strongly to one error, we may actually go too far in the right direction and find ourselves in an opposite error. We were drifting toward a certain ditch, and before we went into it, we jerked the wheel so hard in the other direction that we overcorrected and went into the ditch on the other side. Similarly, we may appreciate a good thing so much that we end up making an idol out of it and end up worshiping it instead of worshiping God. In a way, this is what happened to the idea of faith, which had fallen on rather hard times until roughly five hundred years ago, when a doughty monk named Martin Luther happened to rediscover it.

Luther had lived in a world in which the focus on one's behavior—or on what we call "works"—had become so important that the Church had lost sight of the simple idea that it is not we who save ourselves by our efforts, but God who saves us by His sacrificial death on the Cross. All we need do to be justified is to believe in Him and in what He did. That is our job. If we believe, all else that is necessary will follow. So when Martin Luther established the centrality of faith—and more than the mere centrality but the very *necessity* of faith—to one's salvation, he was doing something vitally important, and it was a bracing corrective to centuries of confusion on the issue. But we should see that in doing this, he opened the door to some other theological troubles.

"By Faith Alone"

The story of Luther and his views on faith and other things are not only central to the German Church during Bonhoeffer's time, but equally central to the American evangelical church of our own day.

As we say, Luther had grown up in a world that had effectively forgotten that we are saved by faith. In the High Medieval church, great corruption had set in, and as a part of the greater mess, any especially scrupulous monk like Martin Luther was essentially encouraged to climb to Heaven via his own efforts. So early on in his life as a young monk, Luther developed a nearly—if not altogether—mad obsession with his own moral perfection. He had been given the idea that it was possible to "work the system" of confession, prayer, and devotion to God in such a way that he really could become blameless, and nothing less was acceptable. This theology had some practical limits, but Luther seemed unable to respect them. So instead of properly focusing on God's love and forgiveness of his sins, he focused on himself and his own efforts—believing that if he did not confess every imaginable sin to his "Father Confessor," those sins clung to him and would drag him to eternal torment in Hell. In other words, they would remain unforgiven.

Luther was so meticulous about this that he believed every conceivable sin of his thoughts must be confessed, and he often spent many hours with his Father Confessor von Staupitz attempting to verbally confess every nuance of every stray and sinful thought. Von

Staupitz tried to get Luther to see where he was going wrong, but in vain. It was as though Luther was somehow determined to clamber up the Tower of Babel into Heaven by his own strength, as though if only he tried harder and harder, he might make it. He prayed and confessed himself half mad, and he did penance and fasted until he was little more than skin and bones. It was only through his repeated failures to succeed in this—and the misery it brought to him—that he finally was obliged to step back and see if he might be missing something.

Eventually, in studying the Scriptures he found the cure for his spiritual malady—and when he found it, he nearly burst for joy. What Luther read not only changed him forever, but through him it changed the world forever. For what he read was that we are not justified by our works, but by our faith. It was simply that simple.

There are many scriptures that make this point clearly. Romans 1:17 says: "For in it the righteousness of God is revealed from faith for faith, as it is written, 'The righteous shall live by faith.'" Romans 5:1 says, "Therefore, since we have been justified by faith, we have peace with God through our Lord Jesus Christ." In Galatians 2:16, we read, "yet we know that a person is not justified by works of the law but through faith in Jesus Christ, so we also have believed in Christ Jesus, in order to be justified by faith in Christ and not by works of the law, because by works of the law no one will be justified."

When we know what agonies Luther endured before he saw this and understood it, we may see why he sometimes almost saw nothing else. Jesus died on the cross for our sins, and when we accept His sacrifice by simple faith, we are saved.

But in his understandably giddy joy, Luther may sometimes have gone a bit farther than necessary, or at least opened the door for others to do so. For example, when he translated Romans 3:28 from the original New Testament Greek into German, Luther added the single

word "alone" to the following sentence: "For we hold that one is justified by faith apart from works of the law." Luther's version was,
"Therefore we conclude that a man is justified by faith *alone* without
the deeds of the law." Luther felt the need to add that word to underscore what for him was essentially the central idea in the universe,
and he may be forgiven for this.

But this tiny two-syllable addition was not the end of the subject.
When translating the entirety of the New Testament into the German
of his day, Luther thought he should leave out the Epistle of James,
since it not only didn't make this point clearly, but almost seemed to
contradict it. In typically Luther-esque fashion, he mocked and
derided the inescapably canonical letter as "an epistle of straw." Eventually he came to change his view, but for a time he really had become
so obsessed with the idea of "faith alone" that James's important
clarification on the subject of faith within the very pages of the Scriptures was suspect. We might say that Luther had in his zeal made an
idol of his idea of faith, so that the genuine faith to which God calls
us was crowded out.

So we should turn to James's epistle, and particularly to the verses
in its second chapter that troubled Luther to such snippy distraction:

> What good is it, my brothers, if someone says he has faith
> but does not have works? Can that faith save him? . . . But
> someone will say, "You have faith and I have works." Show
> me your faith apart from your works, and I will show you
> my faith by my works. You believe that God is one; you do
> well. Even the demons believe—and shudder! Do you want
> to be shown, you foolish person, that faith apart from
> works is useless? Was not Abraham our father justified by
> works when he offered up his son Isaac on the altar? You
> see that faith was active along with his works, and faith

was completed by his works; and the Scripture was fulfilled that says, "Abraham believed God, and it was counted to him as righteousness"—and he was called a friend of God. You see that a person is justified by works and not by faith alone. And in the same way was not also Rahab the prostitute justified by works when she received the messengers and sent them out by another way? For as the body apart from the spirit is dead, so also faith apart from works is dead. (James 2:14, 18–26)

James the brother of Jesus wrote these words to the Jewish believers in the middle of the first century, hardly dreaming that his letter would soon become part of the scriptural canon of the Church for all time. And he could not possibly have imagined that fifteen centuries after he had written it, an overzealous monk would threaten to consign it to the noncanonical limbo of such works as the Shepherd of Hermas. We should be grateful that Luther soon reconsidered his hasty judgment. But we can of course see what troubled him about James's epistle. A bit earlier in it, James wrote, "But be doers of the word, and not hearers only, deceiving yourselves." (1:22). James knew it was easy enough to hear something and nod our assent, but if we do not act on what we have heard, we are deceiving ourselves. There is more to believing than mere intellectual assent. But to Luther, who was essentially obsessed with the idea that we are justified by faith alone, such verses were flies in the ointment. Nonetheless, what James wrote was a necessary corrective to those for whom "faith" had pushed away the vital need actually to do good, and has remained such to this day.

James speaks in a sarcastic and mocking tone to make his point. "You say you believe there is one God," he writes. "You do well. Even the demons believe—and tremble!" In our own language we might say, "You say you believe in God. Good for you! So does Satan!" The clear implication of what James is writing is that God expects infinitely more of us than simply saying we "believe." Many of those to whom he was writing must have been guilty of this misunderstanding of "belief." He makes it clear that the idea that we must only "believe" or "have faith" was self-refuting nonsense, and explains that it is actually what we do that matters, *because our actions illustrate what we actually believe.* So if we do not do good works, we obviously do not have the faith we claim.

This is of course what deeply bothered Luther, so we must be clear. We cannot earn our way into God's good graces by what we do—as though our good works could themselves lift us into Heaven. Of course not. Nonetheless *what* we do shows what we actually believe. So if we do not do those things which proceed from real faith, we cannot simply claim to have faith. If we are not doing the works that naturally proceed from our faith, we manifestly have no faith. And so we are in fact not justified before God, which is a chilling thing to consider.

It's one thing to say that our faith saves us. Luther understood that, and all of the Scriptures attest to it. But if our faith does not manifest itself in good works, then it's obvious we actually have no faith. So those to whom James was writing were getting a bitterly serious warning. If you are under the impression that your "faith" is all you need to get into Heaven, that's fine, because it's true. But you had better be sure that you actually *have* faith, and James's letter was written to make crystal clear that if you do not have works, you must understand that you actually do not have faith—and are therefore not saved at all.

Bonhoeffer in his book *The Cost of Discipleship* makes a very similar and related point about what he calls "cheap grace," which we will touch on shortly. But first, we continue on the subject of those problems that arise from a misunderstanding of "faith."

Faith as a Fig Leaf

Let us now turn to the third chapter of Genesis, where we read the fathomlessly tragic story of our first ancestors, Adam and Eve. This gives us the archetypal and seminal picture of what it looks like when we try to fool God, as when we say we "believe" something but actually do not believe it at all. In the story, we see that when Adam and Eve disobey God, they are immediately aware of what they have done. "Then the eyes of both were opened, and they knew that they were naked. And they sewed fig leaves together and made themselves loincloths." (Genesis 3:7)

It is a strange and impossibly rich picture that God gives us in this single verse. Adam and Eve know they have done wrong, and instantly decide they must remedy it. But why? They suddenly recognize their nakedness, but why do they think they must do anything about it? Many books have been filled with the implications of this, but for our purposes let's simply say they know there is a problem. And what do they do? To cover their nakedness, they resourcefully weave fig leaves together into loincloths of some kind—some translations use the word "aprons"—and that's that. They seem to think these fig-leaf coverings will do the job. They do not ask God what to do, but do this themselves and do it quickly, before He is able to see them as they are.

In paintings, Adam and Eve are typically pictured with a single fig leaf covering their private parts. Many of the nude sculptures during the Renaissance—including Michelangelo's colossal David—were deemed by some to be a bit too realistic, and perhaps in response to the Reformation rocking Europe at that time, some in the Catholic Church thought erring on the side of discretion the thing to do. So these minimalist fig leaf coverings—rather than entire loincloths of fig leaves—were usually employed to cover things up while doing minimal aesthetic harm to the artistic work. But the point of the Genesis story is that mere fig leaves—in any number or formation—are completely insufficient. The fig leaves are Adam and Eve's sad and, in some ways, pathetic attempt to cover their nakedness. It was what we might call "works righteousness," and it would not do. Not at all.

In verse 21, after God has pronounced His judgment upon them, we read: "And the Lord God made for Adam and for his wife garments of skins and clothed them." It is an absolutely extraordinary thing, with the most profound implications: God in this action makes it clear that whatever Adam and Eve had done with their fig leaves was not nearly sufficient. So He Himself had to do what was necessary to cover their nakedness and sin. Suddenly we see that blood had to be shed—and life taken—to cover the problem. It is infinitely worse than Adam and Eve had supposed.

We cannot cover up our nakedness and cannot begin to bridge the divide our sin has created between us and God. God Himself has to do it. So animals had to be killed and blood shed so that their skins could be used for the job of covering. The depth of meaning here is extraordinary, and of course it points to Jesus's death on the cross in the future. But for our purposes let's simply restate the simple fact that Adam and Eve's actions in covering themselves with fig leaves is not merely insufficient, but is actually offensive to God.

We may see their actions in this as constituting the first "religious" act in history. Religion—in the pejorative sense—seems to think that we ourselves can do this or that, or cannot do this or that, and thereby earn our way back into God's good graces by our behaviors. In religious actions, we seek to minimize the horrifying reality of our disobedience, and then cavalierly attempt to bridge the divide ourselves, as if that were possible.

Again, the idea was that Adam and Eve might somehow fool God by covering themselves with fig leaves. They knew enough to feel that something needed doing, but rather than humble themselves before

God and confess that they had disobeyed Him, they compounded their estrangement from Him. God nonetheless provided what was needed, but Adam and Eve's homespun efforts made quite clear that they didn't see the depth and horror of their disobedience.

The point of this for our own purposes here is that when we tell God we believe something we do not truly believe—as James recounts in his letter—we are essentially repeating the actions of Adam and Eve in covering themselves with fig leaves. It is a deception and a lie. We are lying to ourselves in this, but of course we seem to think we can lie to God and fool Him, too. So when we try to fool ourselves—and God—in this way, we do something even deeper and more affronting than our initial sin. It is one thing not to truly believe what God asks us to believe, and to be honest about our disbelief. But it is another thing to say that we do believe when God knows we don't.

Just as Bonhoeffer talks about how the German Church of his time had cheapened the idea of grace unconscionably, so have we in the American Church cheapened the ideas of belief and real faith. James in his epistle is talking to all of us who think there need be no connection between what we say we believe and how we live. We have reduced belief to mere intellectual assent. If someone today is asked what he believes, that person might direct us to read the statement of faith on the website of the church they attend. But to God, that statement of faith is a fig leaf, and a kind of lie. The statement of faith may be perfectly fine, but our claiming that it speaks for us is a laughable attempt to fool God into thinking that we actually believe what that statement of faith says. But of course, God is not fooled. He sees our hearts. And He sees our actions. He knows precisely what we believe by the way we live our lives. So our attempt to say that we intellectually believe something—and there it is in that statement of faith—is heartbreaking to Him. Can we doubt that it also kindles His anger?

Because once again we are playing a game, as though we might fool God. The statement of faith on our church's website—or perhaps the Nicene Creed or even the Bible, for that matter—becomes little more than a fig leaf we use to perpetuate a lie. We think pointing to these things and saying we assent to them will convince God that we actually *do* assent to what they claim. But God knows better. He isn't interested in what we *claim* to believe but in what we *actually believe*. And He sees the difference in our lives. He sees our hearts and observes our actions. And if our actions do not comport with what we claim to believe in that statement or that creed, He knows we are lying to ourselves and to Him, and it breaks His heart.

He wants us to be honest with Him, to trust Him to help us. But instead, we try to justify ourselves. We cover ourselves with the fig leaf of that doctrinal statement or with the whole Bible. But God knows that in this action we actually are building our own Towers of Babel in order to reach Heaven of our own accord. We are foolish enough to think we can do it ourselves, as though the gulf were not infinite. And we are even more foolish in thinking that God will not see what we are really doing.

When the German Church in the 1930s and the American Church of our day focus on doctrinal statements but forget that we are obliged to live out what we claim to believe, we make a mockery of what God actually requires of us. This is what Bonhoeffer was calling the German Church to repent of in his Reformation Day sermon, and it is this that God is calling the American Church to repent of today.

So we must ask ourselves: *Does how I live show God that I actually believe what I claim to believe? Or does how I live show God that actually I do not believe what I claim to believe?* Can we hear the words of James and of Bonhoeffer and admit that we do not have the faith we have claimed to have? Only then—when we see that we do not have it and are therefore not justified—will we humble ourselves and ask God to give us that real faith.

Because God loves us, He is hurt by these things, is heartbroken by them. And it is because He loves us that He is angry at our deception and disobedience. We can imagine Him asking: "How could you? Did you not know that I loved you and would do anything to help you? Did you not know that I would send My only begotten Son to die a torturous death on a Roman cross for your sake? Did that mean nothing to you?" And of course, it is clear by our actions—or by our inaction—that it did not mean anything to us. It is clear we didn't understand what God required of us. We didn't understand that He asks us only to be honest with Him and to trust Him, to show that we love Him and know that He loves us by not trying to fool Him, but by being honest with Him about our own faults and shortcomings and asking for His help.

This is the very place where much of the American Church is today. We point to statements of faith and to creeds and confessions, but God sees our hearts. He sees us shrink from speaking when we should speak, and He knows the real reason behind our silence. He sees whether we believe by what we do and don't do. And if we have attended hundreds of Bible studies and heard hundreds of sermons, it only makes everything much the worse. If we are not actually living out what we claim to know and believe, then we have learned what we have learned and heard what we have heard "to our destruction," in the same way that we drink the body and blood of Jesus cavalierly, in a condition of unconfessed sin and unrepentance. What we claim to believe makes a great claim on us, and God holds us responsible for what we claim to believe and expects us to live it out.

To the extent that the American Church is guilty of this—like the German Church on Reformation Day 1932 and like the church in Ephesus at the end of the first century—we have forgotten our first love. We have drifted from that open and honest relationship with the One who died for us and loves us with an unfathomable love. We have relegated our faith to mere intellectual assent to some words and doctrines, and in doing so—ironically and tragically—we have proved that we do not actually believe those words or those doctrines at all. What could be more heartbreaking to God than that?

Most important of all, we say we believe that Jesus defeated death on the cross. Do others looking at our lives get the impression that we believe that we genuinely do not fear death because we know that Jesus really has defeated it, and not merely as a metaphor? Or do we look like we are hedging our bets? Bonhoeffer knew that the German Church of his day was hedging its bets, and that as a result, they were not doing what God called them to do in their hour of trial.

Chapter Eight

The Church Paralyzed

You see that a person is justified by works and not by faith alone.

—JAMES 2:24

In this final section about the error that comes from misunder-standing what true faith is, we come to that verse in which James wrote that we are "justified by our works, and not by faith only." To Luther, surely this had to be the most nettlesome of all in James's whole unpleasant epistle. Not because Luther didn't understand what James was getting at, but because it could easily be misunderstood as meaning *precisely the opposite* of what Luther with his whole being was trying to say. Luther had so hammered upon the idea of "faith alone" that it had become the battle cry of the Reformation, *Sola Fide*! But this unfortunately created the atmosphere against which Bonhoeffer was preaching that Reformation Day in 1932. For even this good idea can be twisted away from God's purposes and can become an idol.

The phrase "faith alone" had made the Christian faith so simple—and ultimately so thin and one-dimensional—that over time it was easily and blithely assented to by nearly everyone in the German nation, so that Bonhoeffer wrote about it in *The Cost of Discipleship*.

Faith was meant to be expressed by loving God with our whole being, and must not be reduced to an Enlightenment rationalist proposition. As James in his epistle tells us, even the demons "believe" and tremble. So in many ways, it is words that create the problem. We use words like *faith* and *belief,* and over time they come to mean something far less vital than they did in the beginning. So we have to revisit these ideas, and restore the Christian faith to its fullness in the minds of the Church.

Living out our Christian faith is less an issue of what we *believe* than an issue of in *whom we trust.* After all, the devil and demons "believe" in God and despise Him. So the question is whether our belief in God brings us to trust in Him with our whole being. That's what it really means to believe in God.

Another way of looking at the question of what we "believe" comes to us from the author Os Guinness, who in his book *The Great Quest* tells the story of an African Christian discussing the concept of faith in hunting terms. The European idea of "belief" has devolved into an intellectual exercise that may be expressed in the image of a hunter raising his rifle to shoot at a stag from a great distance. But the African way of thinking about faith—which is of course the biblical way of thinking about it—presents us with the much more visceral image of a lion pouncing upon a stag. The lion's whole being is required in the action; its sinews and muscles and bones are all vitally central to the task. But of course, the hunter from a distance only needs to aim and then move his index finger half an inch. We can see why that may somehow be preferable to the lion's approach, but with regard to faith and belief, it is not at all adequate. We need to engage with everything in us.

Jesus in Matthew 22 is asked, "Which is the greatest commandment in the Law?" And He responds: "You shall love the Lord your God with all your heart and with all your soul and with all your mind. This is the great and first commandment."

Can we imagine how far that idea is from our own attenuated ideas of "faith" and "belief"? First of all, it is a commandment. It is not a suggestion. It is utterly required of us. There is nothing sideways about it and no suggestion that it is a suggestion. And the commandment is not that we merely believe in God, but that we *love* Him. Can there be any more astonishing contrast than that between merely "believing" in God and in loving Him? And just in case we have a thin view of what love means, Jesus says that we are to do it with all of our heart and with all of our soul and with all of our mind. Is there any way that we can miss His meaning in that? God commands us to passionately and utterly and wholeheartedly *love* Him. He is not interested in what we say we "believe." He demands from us the wholehearted and passionate devotion of a lover. And if we follow this line of thinking, we will understand that God is jealous for us. He is not indifferent to our indifference. He is not looking for our mere legalistic assent to anything. That intellectual assent is not merely insufficient, but is offensive to Him. He is looking for everything we have to give, for our whole selves, for us and us alone.

The image from Os Guinness's book may be augmented with another.

Let's imagine a high-wire artist who has affixed a cable across a dangerous waterfall and then proceeds to walk back and forth across it. A crowd gathers, of course, and upon returning from his jaunt across the taut wire, the man points to a wheelbarrow and asks the crowd whether they believe he can push it all the way across to the other side. Most people believe that he can, so they nod or even shout, "Yes!" The high-wire artist singles out a man in the front of the crowd, who seemed most confident in answering affirmatively. "You, sir!" the high-wire artist says to the man. "You say you believe that I can wheel the barrow across the cataract. Is that true? Do you really believe it?"

"I do!" the man says.

"Even with a heavy load inside the barrow?"

"Why not? Certainly!"

"Very well," the high-wire artist says, "I'm glad to hear it. So please help me to show everyone else that I can do it by getting into the barrow!"

Suddenly whether the man really and truly believes this can be done has become terribly personal. If he does, he should have no difficulty getting into the barrow. But if he doesn't really and truly believe, he will never get into it.

Isn't that precisely the issue with what we believe? We say we believe that Jesus has defeated death on the Cross. Many of us affirm it when we recite the Nicene Creed. But God knows whether we *actually* believe it or are just claiming to. He sees it by our actions.

God asks us: "Will you trust Me with your income? Will you trust Me with your life? Will you trust Me with your spouse's life or your child's life? Who do you say that I am?"

God is not satisfied—or fooled—by what we say we "believe" any more than the devil is fooled by what we say we "believe." Or any more than our neighbors are fooled, or our friends or enemies. People see precisely what we believe by how we behave. Can there be any doubt that we don't believe much of what we claim to believe? What will it take for us genuinely to believe what God says? What will it take for us to understand that God is not fooled by what we claim to believe?

✻

Bonhoeffer's *The Cost of Discipleship* is most famous for its early chapters, in which he takes the German Church to task for doing something related to and extremely similar to what we have been discussing. He calls it "cheap grace" and says that "cheap grace" is not grace at all. We might say that it is counterfeit grace, or the devil's grace. To treat the limitless and infinitely costly grace of God as something worth very little is to do the ugliest thing imaginable. Cheap grace is like faith that is not really faith but that only pretends to be faith—as if to deceive ourselves and God—and precisely like that, it may creep up on us over time until we have no idea we are guilty of any such thing.

So when Bonhoeffer preached his sermon on Reformation Day in 1932, he was surely thinking about this concept that he would soon enough immortalize in his famous book. He knew that Luther had so succeeded in expressing and popularizing the idea that we are saved by faith—that it is God's grace that does everything, and we who do nothing—that many had really come to believe that nothing was required of them. Their intellectual assent to Jesus's sacrifice was quite enough, and having done that, they could now get on with their lives. So it was no wonder to Bonhoeffer when he preached that day that the church of Luther had become a caricature of itself, and that someone must make this known to those souls sleepwalking toward the abyss, which was far closer than anyone dreamt.

In his book—in German the title is simply *Nachfolge*, which means "discipleship," or literally "to follow after"—Bonhoeffer also talks about the necessity of obedience in the Christian life. To any Lutheran of his day, or to any evangelical today who has been trained to think only in terms of "faith" or "belief," it can be a startling concept. Does Bonhoeffer not know that our "works" are of no use? But of course he knew that just as we may not earn our way to Heaven by our works, neither can we get there without good works—because if we have the faith that will bring us to Heaven, we will inevitably do good works. There was nothing new in this idea since the Bible is quite clear on the subject, as we have already said. But sometimes we need to hear something afresh, and to discover it afresh, just as Luther had to rediscover the idea of "faith" at a time when it was all but lost.

Bonhoeffer's searing words on "cheap grace" could hardly be clearer.

> I can go and sin as much as I like, and rely on this grace to forgive me, for after all the world is justified in principle by grace. I can therefore cling to my bourgeois secular existence, and remain as I was before, with the added assurance that the grace of God will cover me. It is under the influence of this kind of "grace" that the world has been made "Christian," but at the cost of secularizing the Christian religion as never before. The antithesis between the Christian life and the life of bourgeois respectability is at an end. The Christian life comes to mean nothing more than living in the world and as the world, in being no different from the world, in fact, in being prohibited from being different from the world for the sake of grace. The upshot of it all is that my only duty as a Christian is to leave the world for an hour so on a Sunday morning and go to church to be assured that my sins are all forgiven. I need no longer try to follow Christ, for cheap grace, the bitterest foe of discipleship, which true discipleship must loath and detest, has freed me from that.[1]

That was the sum of his indictment of the German Church in his own day. By the time he wrote these words in 1936, he could see the monstrous reality that this cheap grace had wrought in his country, and he would see much more still to come.

---

[1] Dietrich Bonhoeffer, *The Cost of Discipleship* (New York: Macmillan, 1959), 50–51.

But here is the greater horror: his words are an indictment of the American Church today. The only difference between us and the German Church of that time is that we have been able to see what happens when the Church does not do what God calls it to do. We have the example of the German Church in his day as a warning.

Therefore, if we do not rise to the occasion now and do what God asks of us, shall we wonder whose sin is the greater?

Chapter Nine

The Idol of Evangelism

The second error of which we in the American Church have become guilty—and of which many in the German Church were guilty in the 1930s—may be called "the idol of evangelism." In the same way that Luther's zeal for our justification by faith was used to crowd out other essential biblical ideas—and therefore led to theological errors, which may lead to historical tragedy—so can the vital concept of evangelism be gravely misunderstood.

If we elevate any good idea too far, we distort that idea and everything along with it. So just as one might say that "faith" is everything—and thereby forget that "faith" must be lived out with our whole being and manifested in how we behave—one might say that the most important thing in the world is that someone come to salvation. After all, if the infinity of eternity is at stake, nothing can even begin to compare with that level of gravity. And so we go about calculating how to do this one thing and this alone. Not only is this the most important thing imaginable, but we encourage ourselves further with the idea that when someone comes to faith, their behavior and their views on every subject will eventually come into line with God's will. They will instantly come to hold a biblical view of sexuality and of the infinite value of all life, and anything else that is biblical. It's inevitable.

Of course, it's not quite that simple. God expects us, and often calls us, to do many things at once. Discipleship is not evangelism, but if we think that without attending to the serious work of discipleship, we can ever be anything like what God intends for His Church, we are mistaken. Nor does the Bible present us with a picture of God's people doing nothing but leading others to salvation. Sometimes God enjoins His people to build walls or to fight battles. Sometimes He has us say difficult things to people who do not receive those difficult things, but who instead walk away forever. Nonetheless there are some who have this fixed idea that evangelism is the most important and really the only thing worth doing. After all, what's the point in doing anything at all if one more soul ends up in Hell for eternity?

But if we are to take the Bible as a whole, we see that this view is a capacious misunderstanding of what God expects of us—and as with any such misunderstandings, it leads to grave errors and problems, and often to tragedy.

For one thing, it may well cause us never to say anything that might offend someone, because we fear that that offense—on some infinitely less important issue than eternal salvation—might drive that person from assenting to the only thing that matters, which is a "saving faith in Jesus Christ." But if we adopt this myopic and unbiblical view, we will essentially be paralyzed, unable to do any of the many other things to which God calls us. As we have earlier touched on reducing "faith" and "belief" to some thin intellectual assent that misses the heart of what it means to love God with our whole being, we have here similarly reduced the "Gospel" to convincing someone to assent to God's simple plan of salvation. If we are able to get that person to pray a certain prayer, we have done all that is needed and may move on. We can dispense with fighting for justice, or against slavery, or with trying to see that our government enacts the will of the people. We relegate such things to some worldly list of what you can do if you didn't get the memo that the only thing that matters is bringing others to personal salvation. Won't all of that other stuff burn anyway? Why waste our time with any of it?

Of course, as extraordinarily vital as evangelism is, God calls us to more. And in doing those other things, we can rest assured He is using whatever He has asked us to do *for His eternal and evangelistic purposes.* The only caveat is that it will not be so immediately evident to us, and may never be.

God calls us sometimes, for example, "to speak truth to power," and gives us a memorable picture of John the Baptist doing that with Herod as well as the astonishing picture of Jesus doing that with the religious leaders of His time. But if John the Baptist and Jesus only cared about the salvation of those to whom they were speaking, could they have said much of what they said? Obviously, God's calculus is not quite what ours is. But do we dare to think that we care more about souls than God?

For example, Jesus called the Pharisees "white-washed tombs" and said they were "of their father, the devil." John quotes Him as saying,

> "You are of your father the devil, and your will is to do your father's desires. He was a murderer from the beginning, and does not stand in the truth, because there is no truth in him. When he lies, he speaks out of his own character, for he is a liar and the father of lies. But because I tell the truth, you do not believe me. Which one of you convicts me of sin? If I tell the truth, why do you not believe me?

Whoever is of God hears the words of God. The reason
why you do not hear them is that you are not of God."
(John 8:44–47)

Jesus actually tells them that the devil is their father. Can we
imagine anything more aggressive and awful to say? Did Jesus not
realize that anything He said that might be so extremely insulting
could push them away from finding true faith?

But obviously Jesus—who was perfect and sinless—knew more
than a little about what He was doing, and in making these harsh
pronouncements showed us another side of things. He was engaged
in "truth-telling." In its own way, this is part of what will indeed
eventually bring some people to salvation.

We also remember that Jesus turned over the tables of the
moneychangers in the Temple and braided a whip of cords to drive
the animals out while shouting. To many in the Church today this
is the very definition of "toxic masculinity"—and perhaps just as
Luther wished James's epistle had been lost to history, many Christians today secretly wish this unfortunate episode had been kept
out of the Gospels. But far from being a picture of "toxic masculinity," this is a picture of perfect masculinity. It is a picture of
God's idea of masculinity. In this muscular action of some violence,
we have God's own picture of Himself: a holy God who acts in
history, and who sometimes does shocking things out of His love
for us.

Throughout the Old Testament God judges Israel and its people
for their behavior, but can we doubt that He does it out of love for
them? Through the mouths of the prophets, He essentially threatens
them that if they don't do X then Y will happen. And if they do X
then Z will happily result. This is a picture of a father's love, not of
someone who is controlling or egotistical or "agenda-driven." If we

care so much about "leading people to Christ" that we are somehow holier than God Himself, to what God are we leading them?

�֍

Because of this hypertrophied view of evangelism, there are many today who refuse to comment on anything controversial or political if they think it might conceivably interfere with the possibility of leading someone to salvation. They forget that God gives them other duties, including loving our neighbors by sometimes speaking the truth. We become so desperate to show those listening to us that we are exactly like them—and that we do not judge them—that we forget these are not the only things worth being concerned with.

We hear over and over of pastors who have taken this tack with tragic results. The tats and skinny jeans and smoke machines and celebrities in the green room—and all of our professions of "nonjudgmentalism"— are not quite enough to bring people to Jesus. At some point we may be required to say something that causes people to stop nodding along, and might even cause them to walk away. When Jesus spoke of the necessity of us "eating His body" and "drinking His blood," He knew that many would turn away, would say "enough" and go back to their lives without Him. But He said it anyway. We know it was not a mis-calculation on His part. When we wore our bright bracelets that cava-lierly asked "What would Jesus do?" we might have remembered that at a certain juncture, that is precisely what He did. And that people walked away when He did it.

But Jesus trusted His Heavenly Father with the eternal souls of those who could not bear His hard teaching. Do we? Recently we saw a celebrity pastor enjoy extraordinary moments in the media spotlight, but in those moments when it suddenly got real, so to speak, he was unable to be clear about God's most basic views on things like sexual morality, for example. He could not bring himself to say that the Bible has had this view of men and women from the beginning and that Jesus said as much. He was not able to spend some of the good will and hip bona fides he had been accumulating, ostensibly for moments like this. This was the opportunity to spend that coin. But instead, the coin was buried safely.

Have we forgotten that God has given us these coins to spend for His purposes? Has that coin become an idol from which we cannot bear to part? Has it become so valuable to us that it is now controlling us?

Not long after the celebrity pastor's TV appearance alluded to above, we wept to hear that he had fallen into sexual sin and had been living a double life. Our hearts break, because we know that the idol he had unwittingly been worshiping had exacted its tribute from him, and we pray for him.

＊

At least as early as writing "The Church and the Jewish Question," Bonhoeffer saw that those in the Church have a solemn obligation to speak up when they see grave injustices. Some years later, he famously wrote, "Only he who cries out for the Jews may sing Gregorian chants." In other words, we shouldn't imagine that God would have us worship Him and listen to sermons if we have neglected to do what we can to speak for those who cannot speak for themselves.

The idol of evangelism—which is of course really an idol of "false evangelism"—was a great part of what silenced the Church in Germany in the 1930s. We only want to preach the Gospel, many pastors said. So rather than potentially be thrown into prison for speaking the truth of God, they kept their mouths shut, hoping the Nazis would leave them in peace.

But did it ever occur to them that if God allowed them to go to prison or to a concentration camp for obeying Him, perhaps He had someone in one of those places to whom He was sending them? Bonhoeffer shared his faith with innumerable souls at Tegel Prison in Berlin, and then later on in the other places to which he was taken before his death.

✠

Only weeks ago, while attending the National Religious Broadcasters convention, I was in a room with a prominent American pastor who openly shared how proud he was not to have said anything so controversial that he might in any way be "cancelled" or lose his opportunity to "preach the Gospel." For him the price of silence on any number of issues was one he paid with joy if it gave him the opportunity to continue doing what he believed God had called him to do. But what if God had called him to say something that arose from what he believed, but that those who had the power to cancel or attack him didn't like? What if he felt an obligation to speak out on any number of issues which the cultural elites had declared off limits? Why would acceding to such tyranny in a free nation be acceptable, and what gospel did he hope to preach if he was allowing himself to be muzzled in this way? Is it not possible that his witness for the Gospel actually would be strengthened if he dared to say what less timid pastors were afraid to say?

But he had such a theologically narrow view of what it meant to "preach the Gospel" that this had obviously never occurred to him. And as far as he was concerned, those being cancelled were only reaping the results of the imprudence of not keeping focused on their strict evangelistic duties. It never occurred to him that he was helping the enemies of freedom—and the Gospel—gain strength. It never occurred to him that by playing such a game, he was making it more difficult for people in a free society to speak the truth, and that this ability to speak truth freely and without fear is indeed a "Gospel issue."

✳

As we have said, many pastors in Bonhoeffer's day were making a similar calculation, although we are able to see exactly how it played out in the end. Bonhoeffer read of one well-meaning American evangelist—Frank Buchman, who headed the Oxford Group[1]— who wished to get a meeting with Hitler and his top lieutenants with the idea of leading them to faith. But Bonhoeffer knew there comes a point when such things are naïve to the point of being destructive. We know that theoretically there is no length to which we shouldn't go to bring a soul into the Kingdom, but a practical element must enter our thinking—and inevitably does, if we are honest. Unless God Himself speaks to us clearly, we are obliged to make such calculations.

When Bonhoeffer was doing all he could to speak out about what was happening and to wake up the Church to act, he was sometimes met with the abominable theology to which we are here referring. Some German pastors felt they must only be allowed to preach the Gospel and lead people to faith. All else was secondary. But at one point—as we have mentioned—Bonhoeffer summed things up quite clearly. "Only he who cries out for the Jews," he said, "may sing Gregorian chants." In other words, if you are unwilling to show the self-giving *agape* love of Christ by openly risking all you have for the sake of those who are suffering, who have no voice, you are no Christian at all, but a hypocrite

---

[1] An interdenominational Christian organization founded in 1921 which later gave birth to Alcoholics Anonymous

and a fraud. God will reject your worship because the very thing that He required of you, you ignored.

Bonhoeffer was quite clear about Christians who "did business as usual." If one did not have the guts to speak against the evils being committed against the German Jews under Hitler, one had abdicated the right to worship God. Many have heard the apocryphal story of Germans in church singing more loudly to drown out the cries of the Jews passing by in boxcars on a nearby railway line. We don't know if the story is true, but we understand the gist of it. But for many years before Jews were being hauled via train lines to their deaths, most German Christians did nothing. Those were years in which they hoped nothing terrible would happen, but did nothing to prevent terrible things from happening. They sat on their hands. They had church services. Perhaps they prayed. Only Bonhoeffer and a handful of Christians did what God was calling all Christians to do.

But when he heard that Buchman was making great efforts to have a meeting with Hitler and later on with Himmler in the hopes of leading these men to faith, Bonhoeffer knew it was a fool's errand. This was not because he didn't care about the souls of the Nazi high command. Obviously, God sent His Son to die for everyone, and if there were any chance of leading these monsters to repentance and faith, Bonhoeffer would be thrilled to take it if possible. But he also saw that those who were singing this easy evangelistic song were ignorant of the realities at hand. He was not. He knew that the time for action was at hand, that human beings were dying and suffering, and that whatever anyone did had better be what God was calling them to do. It had better not be some zealous religious fool's errand, because innumerable lives were at stake.

This is no less true for us today. If we do not speak out at the injustices we see all around us, to what thin-lipped gospel do we think we are leading anyone? If we believe our own government is looking the other way at certain injustices while boldly making a show of being heroically concerned with others, are we not obliged to point this out?

Our responsibilities as Christians go beyond mere "evangelism." We pretend we would have spoken out for the Jews in Bonhoeffer's day, or that we would have spoken against the slave trade in Wilberforce's day, but are we speaking out today on the issues that are no less important to God in our time? If not, we are deceiving ourselves. But God is not deceived.

On what issues are we ourselves being silent, and for what reasons? The unborn are being murdered and their body parts sold for profit. Are we not to mention this for fear of driving someone away from God? Or do we ourselves not quite believe it or wish to believe it?

Very young children in schools are being fed pernicious ideas on the subject of sexuality—ideas with which their young minds are quite unable to cope, and to which their own parents object.

Older children are being so confused by sexual activists that they agree to have their bodies mutilated, so that they can never become the men and women God has created them to be.

Socialistic and communistic ideas are being pushed everywhere. These will end up harming the poor more than anyone, although those pushing these ideas boldly spread the lie that any who oppose these wicked ideas secretly hate the poor.

Are we really to keep silent about all of these things? Is it not possible that those whom we wish to evangelize are looking to us in the Church—who claim to have no fear but of God—to speak boldly on these things and fight for the truth as we see it while there is yet time? Is this not perhaps the very thing that will lead these souls to the God we worship, if we obviously so love Him that we are willing to live in this way?

Chapter Ten

Speaking the Truth in Love

When Pilate immortalized the question "What is truth?" he did so by asking it of the One who Himself was truth. The irony is so painful as to be piercing. But Pilate was doing what leading figures sometimes do: they say something far more profound than they can hope to realize, just as when Caiaphas asked, "Do you understand that it is better for you that one man should die for the people, not that the whole nation should perish?" It seems clear that these men "knew not what they said," and had no idea that God was using them in their historic roles to prophetically speak truths of which they themselves were utterly and tragically unaware.

But Pilate's infamous question comes to us. Do *we* know what truth is? Do we understand that truth and facts are not the same thing? Do we understand that truth is something so illimitably large and fathomless that it created the universe with a word, that it stands outside time and space, that it is a Person? Can we bear the answer to the question "What is truth?"

But somehow God—by taking on human form—asks us to bear it. He asks us to look to Jesus, who somehow in the lowly form of a man is yet God—to see the One who is Truth, to see Him as the standard bearer, and as the standard too. He is an image of truth itself, a battle flag for truth. His is the standard raised up amidst the choking smoke and deafening carnage of the battle between truth and lies. And we are to rally to that battle flag, to Jesus Himself.

So if Jesus Himself is Truth, then what? Then we know that statements of doctrine are not enough. Jesus is alive. Jesus is eternal and immortal. There is something far more to Truth than ideas. If Jesus really is Truth, then we know that truth inescapably partakes of love. The Bible tells us that God is love. So the One who is Truth is also the One who is Love, and it is not possible to separate them without degrading each of them—nor does God wish for us to try. Indeed, we must know that He is deeply grieved if we try to separate them in any way, which we often do. They are part of the very same thing, and by coming to us in human form God is making plain to us that our fallen human attempts to parse truth into something less than the Person of Jesus is to fall into the trap of reductionism. Just as we cannot contain the universe in a nutshell, neither can we reduce truth to syllogisms or even to creeds or confessions. God forbid.

So Truth is a Person. And God knows that unless we understand this, we have no idea what truth is. And unless we know that truth is inextricably intertwined with love, we also have no idea what truth is. Finally, unless we also know that love is inextricably intertwined with truth, we have no idea what love is. We always and ever stray from God in attempting to dissect truth or love in this way, and in so doing we must kill it every time. To follow the parallel, we crucify God every time. It is nothing less than sin to try to have our own fallen view of truth apart from love or love apart from truth. God demands that we deal with the whole, that we understand Truth and Love are

God Himself, who is a Person. Of course, there is profound mystery here, but God requires us sometimes to deal with mystery.

Our Enlightenment minds cannot abide mystery. We have drunk the rationalist Kool-Aid and have in God's own Church introduced the idea that His great and unfathomable mysteries can be reduced to creeds or statements of faith—as if we could reduce Him to that level, as if we could remake Him in our own image, as if we could have truth and love on our own syllogistic, bullet-point terms. After all, it's so much neater than having a relationship with a Person.

But that is what God asks of us. Truth and love are united in Him. To declare any truth in a way that steps away from God's love is to speak no truth at all, as well as to step away from the One who is Truth. But to claim we are being loving when we step away from the Truth of God is not to love at all, but only to fool ourselves into thinking we are being loving. It is also to step away from the One who is Love. And when we "love" in this fallen human way, we are not blessing those whom we claim to be "loving," but are in fact cursing them and damning them. There's no way around it. So not to speak an uncomfortable truth to someone who needs to hear it—and giving the excuse that we are loving them—is not to love them but to harm them.

So we see there are two ways in which someone can err. One is to speak so much "truth" with so little love that he is not actually speaking truth. We have seen and heard such persons, so obsessed with "truth" that whether they are actually communicating success-fully seems immaterial to them. And actually, that's quite the case. They are obviously more concerned with justifying themselves, with proving they are uncompromising purveyors of "truth," than with actually pur-veying truth. They seem to believe they are earning points with whatever god they are serving by such behavior. They are not at all worried about pushing others away with what they are saying. Perhaps they even delight in the idea. But if one is actually communicating—or wanting to communicate—one is naturally not insensitive to whether what one is saying is actually getting across to the person or people with whom one is speaking. That lies at the heart of what it means to speak and communicate.

The opposite of this is an equal problem: to show so much "love" that you are misrepresenting the real love of God, and are forsaking God's truth in the process. You are so afraid of saying something that might push away the one to whom you are speaking that you cease to say anything at all controversial or potentially disagreeable.

Bonhoeffer witnessed this when he first came to the United States in 1930. His fellow students at Union Theological Seminary seemed less interested in what he saw as truth than in some larger truth they believed more important, as though truth had become the hopelessly outdated obsession of the "fundamentalists" of that time. Bonhoeffer was hardly an American fundamentalist, but neither could he make sense of how the "progressive" American Christians of his time could take the fundamentals of the faith so lightly. He saw in time that many of them could do so because they had already dismissed them; such doctrines as the Resurrection and the Atonement were no longer taken seriously.

Sometimes there's nothing wrong with wishing to avoid controversy. We are hardly called to constant contentiousness. The Scriptures talk about being "at peace with all men" and about "becoming all things to all peoples" so that Christ can be made known. But at what point do our efforts in this direction begin to backfire? At what point does our obligation to speak truth give way to what the Bible calls "fear of man"? Proverbs 29:25 says, "The fear of man lays a snare, but whoever trusts in the Lord is safe."

So how has it happened that the secularists have so effectively caricatured Christians as "Bible-thumping moralists" that many

Christians have internalized these criticisms and no longer feel the freedom to speak? How many Christians—and Christian pastors and leaders—are paralyzed for fear that they might say something to drive away the person with whom they are speaking?

We are obliged to wonder: Where are all of the leading American pastors today on the issues of sexuality and transgender madness? Are they afraid to speak? Do they not know that God has appointed them to speak on these issues fearlessly—as though He really has defeated death on the Cross and has freed them to do His will and share His love, come what may?

The first pages of Genesis declare that God created us male and female in His image. Can anything be simpler? Not to aver this at a time when it is being madly challenged—to the detriment of millions of souls—is to be silent in the face of evil, and therefore to partake in evil. Everyone in the world knows that a rooster cannot lay an egg and that a man cannot have a womb—and cannot menstruate or give birth or lactate or be a mother. But who will say it? Who will help lead the way through the carnage of this ideological warfare? Who will hold up the battle standard—which is Jesus Himself—so that others can see and follow?

Young women dedicate their whole beings to athletic excellence, only to be roughly shoved aside in what ought to be their long-awaited moment of triumph by a man who, to the applause of a hopelessly confused and broken culture, claims suddenly to be a woman. A young man is confused about his sexuality, but he only hears one message: that he must seize and celebrate his same-sex attractions as a gift from God. Is your pastor talking about these things? Are you?

✳

We must be honest and admit that much of the time we are not living out our faith but are at least partially enslaved to public opinion over the truth. And this is the main reason we are silent when we should not be silent.

Do we fear that someone will think less of us if we say that we believe sex is made by God for men and women in lifelong marriage? Have we perhaps halfway been persuaded that this idea is outdated enough that it's worth keeping silent about? Are we afraid that someone in a sexual relationship will feel judged by us, and will see us as religious legalists rather than as loving and compassionate followers of Jesus? At what point does our silence encourage someone along in their sin and in their path away from God?

Are we afraid to say that abortion is morally wrong, and that under no circumstances must we equivocate on it? Would we have spoken against slavery in 1850? Would we have spoken against the monstrously antisemitic actions of the Nazis in 1933? Why do we believe we would have spoken then if we are silent now?

If someone in 1975 or 1985 or 1995 or 2005 spoke about sexuality from a biblical viewpoint, and did so in love, the outcry against them would have been minimal. It was the time to speak. And of course it was vital that our words be seasoned with compassion. But it is because of what we earlier described as the "Spiral of Silence" that it is so difficult to speak now. Shall we arrest the downward spiral, or will we go along with it until we can say nothing about anything? Are we not already very close to that? Will we repent of our role in bringing things to this pass?

Again, we may take Bonhoeffer as our model. In his book *Ethics*, which he saw as his magnum opus and which he worked on near the end of his life, he touches on the touchy subject of abortion.

Destruction of the embryo in the mother's womb is a violation of the right to live which God has bestowed upon this nascent life. To raise the question whether we are here concerned already with a human being or not is merely to confuse the issue. The simple fact is that God certainly intended to create a human being and that this nascent human being has been deliberately deprived of his life. And this is nothing but murder.[1]

But Bonhoeffer was not some cold-hearted activist. He was a pastor and a man of God. He saw that there was more to the story, and says so:

> A great many different motives may lead to an action of this kind; indeed in cases where it is an act of despair, performed in circumstances of extreme human or economic destitution and misery, the guilt may often lie rather with the community than with the individual. Precisely in this connection money may conceal many a wanton deed, while the poor man's more reluctant lapse may far more easily be disclosed.[2]

So Bonhoeffer spoke the truth about abortion, but did so with compassion and love. But he did not allow his compassion and his love to silence him on the facts. To be clear about the fact that love and truth are unavoidably connected, he ends his rumination with the following:

> All these considerations must no doubt have a quite decisive influence on our personal and pastoral attitude towards the

---

[1] Dietrich Bonhoeffer, *Ethics* (New York: Touchstone, 1995), 174.
[2] Eric Metaxas, *Bonhoeffer: Pastor, Martyr, Prophet, Spy* (Nashville, TN: Thomas Nelson, 2010), 472.

person concerned, but they cannot in any way alter the fact of murder.[3]

Will we model our public witness on Bonhoeffer in this way? By God's grace, let us do so.

---

[3] Ibid.

Chapter Eleven

Be Ye Not Political

Let every person be subject to the governing authorities. For there is no authority except from God, and those that exist have been instituted by God. Therefore whoever resists the authorities resists what God has appointed, and those who resist will incur judgment. For rulers are not a terror to good conduct, but to bad. Would you have no fear of the one who is in authority? Then do what is good, and you will receive his approval, for he is God's servant for your good. But if you do wrong, be afraid, for he does not bear the sword in vain. For he is the servant of God, an avenger who carries out God's wrath on the wrongdoer. Therefore one must be in subjection, not only to avoid God's wrath but also for the sake of conscience. For because of this you also pay taxes, for the authorities are ministers of God, attending to this very thing. Pay to all what is owed to them: taxes to whom taxes are owed, revenue to whom revenue is owed, respect to whom respect is owed, honor to whom honor is owed.

—ROMANS 13:1–7

If any of the four errors we are discussing could most easily be pushed to the fore in the Germany of the 1930s, it is the idea that Christians ought not to be political. In our own day it is a similarly central error, one that we hear again and again. Of course, there is some truth in every lie, and so we happily acknowledge the truth that we Christians mustn't be *overly* political, to the point where we put our hopes in politics and not in God Himself. We mustn't make an idol out of any good thing, and of course that includes politics. Chuck Colson often made this point by saying that Jesus was not returning to us on Air Force One, which is true. But where did the Church ever get the idea that it was possible to avoid being political at all?

As we have said, not to stand against slavery in Wilberforce's time would have certainly been against God's will, but to stand against it meant being decidedly political. There is no way around it. Doing God's will sometimes entails entering the world of politics, whether we wish to or don't. Standing up for the unborn or for any persecuted group will likely mean being somehow political. So when God's enemies shout that we mustn't be political, as though this constitutes some trump card that can be used against those who claim to be Christians, we are obliged to hear in these cynical cries the voice of the devil, who similarly tried to keep Wilberforce from doing God's will through politics and who has tried to keep God's people from doing good at many times in history. At each of these junctures some Christians have fallen for this ploy and have allowed themselves to be silenced and neutralized, to the great harm of many of their fellow human beings—just as is happening today.

But to understand the roots of this unbiblical idea, we again have to go back to the time of Martin Luther, from whom the Germans of Bonhoeffer's time got the idea. As we know, Luther got much right, but he got some things quite wrong too. Even some of the things he got right eventually went wrong, as circumstances changed over time. Just as his overemphasis on faith and grace led by Bonhoeffer's time to the cheapening of those ideas, so his views on the Church and the state were also eventually far from what they had been in his own time. But Luther cast such a shadow over Germany and the Lutheran church that it was usually asking too much for most Lutheran pastors to question anything he had said, or even to reevaluate it. And that was the problem. Bonhoeffer himself once said if the German Church were to make an idol, it would have precisely the image and form of Martin Luther.

To review Luther's views on this subject, we must revisit the societal turmoil that led to what we now call the Peasant's Revolt, which took place in the 1520s. It was a gruesome chapter in which many Germans were misled to violence against their rulers by their own zealous misapplications of what they believed must follow their new "Lutheran" beliefs. But Luther himself was horrified by it and denounced their violence as boldly as he might—indeed, many thought him far too harsh in this. But to make his point that these peasants had no business attacking their earthly rulers, he put an extremely strong emphasis on those verses quoted above from the thirteenth chapter of Romans. In fact, he made his points so strongly—as Luther was wont to do—that those verses practically eclipsed all else that the Scriptures had to say on the subject for the next four centuries.

Romans 13 begins, "Let everyone be subject to the governing authorities, for there is no authority except that which God has established. The authorities that exist have been established by God." Luther was a combative figure, so when he learned of the tremendous violence being done by those claiming his own teachings as their impetus, he responded with these verses in the strongest terms possible. For him the Scripture was clear as crystal, and for these peasants to violently attempt to overthrow their secular rulers was unmistakably wrong. Under the circumstances in which he found himself, Luther was mostly right, but this thinking in effect became part of the institutional thinking of the German Lutheran church. So that when the brutal and decidedly anti-Christian Nazis claimed to be the "governing authorities" in Germany, the German Church largely fell in line, as though standing against the wicked tyranny of Hitler was obviously and unavoidably wrong.

Of course the reality is more complicated, and the German Church was not schooled in the nuances around this subject. For them it really was that simple. Because Luther had thunderously underscored and proclaimed Romans 13 as the answer on these questions, that settled the issue for the German Lutheran church. So when Hitler came to power, the instinct among German Lutherans was to treat him as they had previously treated the kaiser.

But what was the context of Paul's letter to the Romans? Obviously it was more complicated than Luther had made it sound back in the 1520s. At that point the German princes may have been out of touch with the demands of those over whom they ruled, but they were hardly despots and monsters. Luther was hoping to get the radicals who were raising hell in his name to tone things down, and to understand that waging violence against one's rulers was not to be the first response to their perceived injustices.

In any case, the German tradition of an amicable relationship between church and state had gone on for some time. The kaisers had been openly and happily Christian. So the German Church didn't understand what we who live in America understand: that when the lines are blurred between church and state, it can lead to very bad things. They had particular difficulty in looking beyond what had become the well-established Lutheran theological box.

But four hundred years after Luther, when God looked to His Church to stand against the great evil that had come upon Germany and that would devastate much of the world and murder millions, they balked, using as their chief excuse this outdated application of Paul's words from two millennia before. They felt religiously justified in doing nothing, and the unprecedentedly evil results of their pious inaction would make the world gasp. Indeed, the world gasps to this day, as it struggles to take in how it is possible that a nation ostensibly Christian could have in any way allowed such things to take place.

But what about us? Haven't we in the American Church swallowed these same lies, and haven't we been similarly silenced from speaking and acting boldly against what we see happening in our own time if what we say and do is characterized as "political"? How else can we have allowed things to get to the point where they now are in American society?

We are obliged to speak up despite whether the wider culture applauds or denounces us. When patriotic Americans are unfairly demonized as "white supremacists," are we not obliged to stand up for them just as we are obliged to stand up for those victims of racism in our past? Can we pretend that God is a respecter of persons, or that He is not colorblind and will look the other way when we only defend those whom secular elites deem it fashionable to defend? Shall we not be ashamed of ourselves for being silent when any injustices are allowed to persist because of our fear and silence?

There are currently a host of grave matters that require our attention and for which we will almost certainly be attacked by secular and political foes as being political, and for which many within the Church will attack us for not being focused on "the Gospel" when we raise them. For example, the Church has always held that life in the mother's womb is sacred. This is a nonnegotiable, and when the government makes a law declaring the murder of the unborn child legal, it is not possible for the Church to remain silent. The Church has always known and always held that marriage is a sacred institution, created by God for a man and a woman. When the state attempts to redefine marriage, it is the Church's solemn duty to speak out against this immoral and unnatural law and not to accede to the accusations that we are being bigoted or unloving in so doing. On the contrary, we are obliged for the love of God and our fellow man to say what the Bible says and what the Church has for all of its history taught.

The Church has always known and held that sex is made for marriage, and that when God created mankind in His image, He created us male and female. When the state attempts to upend this eternal order, it is the Church's duty to speak out. Has your pastor spoken out on these issues so that those in the congregation and beyond know that he is not silently assenting to the sweeping changes being proposed? Speaking the truth of God for His purposes is simply our duty. It is not extra-credit Christianity; it is basic Christianity. Actually, it is simply Christianity.

✳

As we have said, the idea that Christian truth—or truth itself—is political is a subjective and meaningless statement, and is in fact designed to silence truth. We see how true this is when people of faith advocate for things that are culturally fashionable and are not challenged for being political. If Christians talk about such issues as human trafficking or racial injustices, their activism is hailed as the very kind of thing they ought to be doing. But if they in a principled way stand up for the unborn, they are libeled as somehow being backward regarding women's rights. Not long ago, a well-known Christian rapper strongly supported a senatorial candidate who holds pro-abortion views as extreme as anyone might imagine, but since the political activism redounded to the benefit of abortion advocates, secularists and political liberals never questioned it. The musician had every right to advocate for whomever he pleased, as we all do in America—but when someone advocates for a candidate so opposed to the idea that life in the womb is sacred, will the Church not speak up about it? As it happens, the Church did not speak up about it, and that candidate became a member of the United States Senate, where he is now forcefully advocating for what Bonhoeffer did not hesitate to call "murder."

In the end, we must only worry about what God thinks of what we say. We must look to Him and to Him alone—else we are in no wise free, but are in bondage to the spirit of the age in which we live. So if someone attacks us for being political, we must cheerfully ignore their criticism. To allow the voices of this world to silence us in this way is precisely how the German Church was silenced.

We may remind ourselves that Jesus had critics who hated Him and what He proclaimed too, and that those critics were motivated by the devil himself to use whatever they could against Him. Logic and truth were not involved in what they said.

> "To what then shall I compare the people of this genera-
> tion, and what are they like? They are like children sitting
> in the marketplace and calling to one another,
> "'We played the flute for you, and you did not dance;
> we sang a dirge, and you did not weep.'
> "For John the Baptist has come eating no bread and
> drinking no wine, and you say, 'He has a demon.' The Son
> of Man has come eating and drinking, and you say, 'Look
> at him! A glutton and a drunkard, a friend of tax collectors
> and sinners!' Yet wisdom is justified by all her children."
> (Luke 7:31–35)

Jesus knew that it was ultimately a spiritual battle, and that we must expect to be criticized and reviled—and to be hated. For they hated Him first. So when we are criticized and called names, we should praise God, who allows us to participate in what He is doing on our planet in our time. We do not deserve this extraordinary honor, but God Himself has graciously given it to us—to you and to me. Shall we decline to accept it?

✳

When Bonhoeffer said that God means the Church to be the conscience of the state, he made it clear that the Church must exist apart from the state and must be free to criticize the state if necessary. When the Church shrinks from this duty—to God and to its fellow citizens—it is not behaving as God's Church. And when that happens, the state and everyone in it will suffer.

In Proverbs 24:11–12, God tells us:

> Rescue those who are being taken away to death;
> hold back those who are stumbling to the slaughter.
> If you say, "Behold, we did not know this,"
> does not he who weighs the heart perceive it?
> Does not he who keeps watch over your soul know it,
> and will he not repay man according to his work?

Where is the caveat that we are not to do these things if someone deems them "political"?

Bonhoeffer eventually became so disgusted with the simplistic Lutheran idea that Christians should not be political that in *The Cost of Discipleship*, he wrote:

> It is high time we broke with our theologically based restraint towards the state's actions—which, after all, is only fear. "Speak out for those who cannot speak." Who in the church today realizes that this is the very least the Bible requires of us?[1]

---

[1] Quoted in Eric Metaxas, *Bonhoeffer: Pastor, Martyr, Prophet, Spy* (Nashville, TN: Thomas Nelson, 2010), 246.

Bonhoeffer became so frustrated with the inability of his fellow German Christians—and even and especially of many in the Confessing Church—to take the bold stand necessary that he began to despair of ever seeing progress and wondered if somehow those who were outside the Church could help those inside it to wake up. Perhaps those outside the Church would not have "theologically based restraint" but would simply see what was right and do it. In the end, in joining the conspiracy to assassinate Hitler, he was decidedly stepping outside the Church—but it was precisely so that he could more freely do precisely what he believed God had called him to do.

But long before he took this step, he was thinking along similar lines when he planned to visit Gandhi in India. Although he was unable actually to make the trip, Bonhoeffer nonetheless saw Gandhi's dedication to resisting colonial tyranny through nonviolent principles—inspired by the Sermon on the Mount—as heroic. So he wondered if he might learn something from this. In a speech at Fanø in Denmark, he asked his Christian audience: "Must we be put to shame by the non-Christian people in the East? Shall we desert the individuals who are risking their lives for this message?"

We hear the urgency in his message. Many were that moment risking their lives while many Christians at conferences such as the one at which he was speaking were dithering, unable to act when the opportunity was so pressing.

Today in America too often we see those who are not at all "Christians" who nonetheless seem to see precisely what is happening and have the courage to speak out. Some of these are simply patriots who love their country, who see that wicked forces are trying to destroy it. Some of them are self-described feminists, who see that a war is being waged on women. These good Americans see that these wild, anarchic forces are working hard to abolish the God-given freedoms enshrined in our founding documents and to upend nearly every aspect of American society—a society that has been the envy of much of the world, going back at least to Tocqueville, who visited here in 1830.

Many of these who are outside the Church see the injustice and madness and know they must fight it—and they are fighting it. They see that these forces want to wipe away the distinctions between men and women, to wipe away any semblance of clarity about sexual behavior and to introduce alien sexual ideas to our children, and they know something is wrong. They do not need to attend church or to read the Bible to see these things.

They have seen that half-mad abortion activists are wildly keening about the "right" to kill children in the womb as though this were a sacred and a good thing, and have witnessed all kinds of powerful forces in government, media, Big Tech, and Big Pharma attempting to silence anyone who dares to voice any disagreement with what these radical elites have declared as the only opinions worth allowing. They have seen these elites not just cancel those who disagree, but have seen them demonize anyone *who does not agree with them loudly enough.* They see an astonishing attack on the values and virtues most Americans cherish—not merely serious Christians, but many devout Jews and Muslims, and many too who rarely mention God. These people are somehow not crippled into silence and inaction by the strange "theology" of many Christians, and so they are leading the way, bravely speaking up and taking the slings and arrows that come with doing so.

That's because truth is truth. There is no "Christian truth." All truth is God's truth, and sometimes it is those who are not bound up and crippled by entangling and confused "religious" views who can see most clearly. They have no strange theological ideas hindering them from speaking out about what they see. They have never been told they mustn't say that the emperor has no clothes—and so they say so, blissfully unaware that some mistakenly believe Romans 13 makes silence on this and other issues the only safe biblical option.

Chapter Twelve

Who Do You Say God Is?

"We do not know what to do, but our eyes are on you."

—2 *CHRONICLES* 20:12

Bonhoeffer's disgust with the German Church's "theologically based restraint" was of course mainly that it was bad theology. It was wrong. He was also disgusted that his fellow German Christians—including those in the Confessing Church—could be so theologically fussy and slow to act when so many were suffering. He was disgusted by the fact that when the German Christians had the opportunity to do something, they didn't. They debated and dithered, as we have said.

The question for each of us in moments of crisis is: *Who do we say that God is?*

Is God a harsh Judge or a loving Father? Because based on our answer to who we believe Him to be, we will answer the other most vital question: *What price are we willing to pay to do the right thing?*

We know that Bonhoeffer's answer to the latter question was that he was willing to pay with his life. We often think this is the ultimate sacrifice. But there is more we can offer before our physical lives are taken from us, if such is to be. That's because when we follow God, we risk the pain of other kinds of deaths before our physical death. For example, we may risk being misunderstood or even vilified by those we have known as allies, or even our dearest friends. As ever, Jesus is the premier example in this, being betrayed in His darkest hour by the man with whom he had spent nearly every day of the previous three years, Judas Iscariot—who not only delivered Him to His enemies and tormentors, but did so with a kiss.

In the end, we are alone with God and His judgment of us. Is God enough?

And what is God asking us to do? What does He think of what we are doing or not doing, or saying or not saying? These are the questions. Is what He thinks enough, or must we have the approval of those others too? Are we willing to pay such a steep price? Or shall we hang back?

If we aren't sure what to do, to whom do we look for answers? Second Chronicles 20:12 is the verse Franz Hildebrandt used in his memorial sermon three months after Bonhoeffer's death: "We do not know what to do, but our eyes are on you."

In *The Cost of Discipleship*, Bonhoeffer writes powerfully about Christ's unequivocal command to love our enemies, to pray for those who persecute us and revile us. He had been forming his thoughts about what he wished to say in the book since 1932. So in 1939, when he made his dramatic decision to return from the safety of the United States to Germany and to join the conspiracy against Hitler—to become dedicatedly "political"—he knew many would misunderstand him. And of course, the resistance to Hitler that expressed itself in that conspiracy was not only political, but had as its goal the violent act of assassinating him along with his top lieutenants. Bonhoeffer knew that very, very few would ever be able to comprehend his decision to become involved in such a conspiracy. He knew they were stuck in continuing to do things as they always had done, not seeing that God Himself called them to respond to the dramatically changed situation. For it is in this way, among others, that we are "wise as serpents."

Often after giving talks on my own book about Bonhoeffer, I have been asked how a man of God such as he could possibly have become involved in anything that involved killing anyone. The naïveté of the question has always made me cringe, knowing that Bonhoeffer himself must have dealt with it, and must have been pained at the naïveté of those who were Christians. First of all, the command in scripture to "Do no murder" did not and could not mean that all killing was murder. To kill in self-defense or to kill during a time of war is quite different from murdering someone. And Bonhoeffer understood that to eschew violence whenever possible did not mean that it was always possible. He knew that as Germany lurched toward war and as Hitler's power became near total, the cost of lives would be staggering. It was already horrific, and he knew about it. So to do nothing would implicate him in real murders—the murders of millions of Jews and others. He was too wise to think he could somehow hang back and do nothing and be absolved of the murders of those millions.

In the end Bonhoeffer knew that he must trust God with the details, with the outcome, and with the judgments of his friends and of history because there was no middle ground, no way to hedge his bets. There was no neutral stand. If he declined to participate in the conspiracy against Hitler, he knew he would unavoidably be helping Hitler execute his satanic plans, which included erasing from the face of the planet the tribe of the Jews, whom Bonhoeffer knew to be God's chosen people.

But he also knew he might be mistaken. Many would have counseled him then—and many take this view today—that it is better to be safe than sorry. It is better to hang back if one is not perfectly sure one is making the right decision. But Bonhoeffer saw the error in this thinking. He knew that such a view was more focused on himself than on those whose lives might be at stake. To love unreservedly—which is God's call to us—is to risk everything, our lives and our reputations. Bonhoeffer's view of God's real grace made it possible for him to trust Him completely. As long as he earnestly desired to do God's will and acted from that motive, he knew the God of the Bible would see his heart and grant him grace, if it happened that he had erred.

So the question comes to us today: Do we believe God looks on our hearts and sees our intentions as they really are, and will forgive us if we make a mistake when our hearts are in the right place? Do we believe He expects us to do the hard thing and not the easy thing—to step out in faith though we will be reviled by our brethren?

This brings us to Jesus's Parable of the Talents, which helps us answer these questions.

Chapter Thirteen

The Parable of the Talents

"For it will be like a man going on a journey, who called his servants and entrusted to them his property. To one he gave five talents, to another two, to another one, to each according to his ability. Then he went away. He who had received the five talents went at once and traded with them, and he made five talents more. So also he who had the two talents made two talents more. But he who had received the one talent went and dug in the ground and hid his master's money. Now after a long time the master of those servants came and settled accounts with them. And he who had received the five talents came forward, bringing five talents more, saying, 'Master, you delivered to me five talents; here, I have made five talents more.' His master said to him, 'Well done, good and faithful servant. You have been faithful over a little; I will set you over much. Enter into the joy of your master.' And he also who had the two talents came forward, saying, 'Master, you delivered to me two talents; here, I have made two talents more.' His master said to him, 'Well done, good and faithful servant. You have been faithful over a little; I will set you over much. Enter into the joy of your master.' He also who had received the one talent came forward, saying, 'Master, I knew you to be a hard man, reaping where you did not sow, and gathering where you scattered no seed, so I was afraid, and I went and hid your talent in the ground. Here, you have what is yours.' But his master answered him, 'You wicked and slothful servant! You knew that I reap where I have not sown and gather where I scattered no seed? 'Then you ought to have invested my money with the bankers, and at my coming I should have received what was my own with

interest. So take the talent from him and give it to him who has the ten talents. For to everyone who has will more be given, and he will have an abundance. But from the one who has not, even what he has will be taken away. And cast the worthless servant into the outer darkness. In that place there will be weeping and gnashing of teeth.'"

—MATTHEW 25:14–30

Jesus's Parable of the Talents is a powerful illustration of what God thinks of our "safe" and "religious" reasons for not doing the right thing, and succinctly expresses the dilemma Bonhoeffer faced, and that we face today.

The question Jesus asks of us in this parable is: "Who do we say God is?" Is He someone we love and trust and know to be a God of grace toward us, or is He rather a "hard master" who can be counted on to punish us if we make a mistake or fail in some way? Jesus makes it plain that those servants who risked the talents they were given were rewarded for doing what they did, and that the servant who "played it safe" by burying the talent was roundly condemned.

Here too we see there is no safe middle path. Jesus abundantly praises the servants who risked what they were given, and unequivocally condemns the servant who has played it safe. But why? For one thing, Jesus is saying that to play it safe is not to play it safe at all. There is no safe option and if you pretend there is, you are deceived and a liar. Either you deem God to be a grace-shedding God or you condemn Him as a hard taskmaster. You must own up to your choice. You cannot have it both ways.

Jesus is telling us that God is a loving God whom we can trust, even if we make mistakes. The question is whether we know and trust Him to be loving, and trust Him so much that we are not frightened in doing something like risking the money He has given us. If we really love Him back, we will do whatever we can to take what He has given us and make it grow. It's obvious that neither of the servants who did this were doing something crazy. They weren't gambling foolishly, for which God would condemn them, but were treating their master's money as though it were their own. If it really had been their own money, they knew that they could make it grow by "trading with it" and promptly did so.

Jesus tells us in the Golden Rule that we are to "Do unto others as we would have them do unto us." And this is an example of that. To truly love someone is to "do unto them as we would have them do unto us." These servants loved their master enough that they were willing to do with his money what they would have done with their own. Their master's true nature enabled them to do this. He freed them to take risks, knowing this is what he would have wanted them to do. He trusted them to do that, and they trusted him to trust them.

Of course we notice that Jesus does not tell the servant who played it safe that he might have done better. On the contrary, he unequivocally condemns him. He seems to be saying that that servant is not under grace, because by treating his master as someone who is not full of grace but is a harsh master, he has put himself out of the reach of that master's grace.

In some ways it is a chilling parable. Jesus seems to be saying, "If you treat me and my Father as though we are 'hard masters,' we will actually be hard masters. The choice is yours. I have made you in my image with full freedom, and when you act as though I am a hard master you actually make me into that hard master. You have that power. You chose the God whom you chose, and that God is your God. Have you chosen the true God, or a counterfeit? If you have chosen the counterfeit, behold, you have chosen Satan. You have chosen freely and will live with your choice." What could be more chilling?

So there is no middle road, no safe road. Jesus is saying that you either know Him and love Him and trust Him—because you know that He loves you and trusts you—or you do not. Jesus was always discerning the hearts of those to whom he spoke, and it is precisely what He does in these parables. He sifts our hearts and divines our intents in a way that reveals Him to be no less than God, which can be frightening. It is certainly amazing. He is God. He knows our hearts. We cannot fool Him.

In Jesus's parables, He forces us to see ourselves and forces us to declare ourselves. Whose side are we on? We have only the two choices. There is no middle ground, and if we try to take that middle ground, we stand condemned. In this parable of the talents, the choice is clear. Either we rejoice in God and love Him and trust Him or we do the very opposite and side with His enemies, judging him as "hard" and behaving in a way calculated not to entrust ourselves to Him. We do not bless Him by our behavior, but protect ourselves *from* Him. In other words, if we do not see Him to be our loving Father, we adjudge him to be someone more like the devil, or indeed, actually to be the devil. If we see him as "religious" and "legalistic" and moralistic, the power He has given us by making us in His image actually enables us to make Him into that other thing. As we judge Him, we judge ourselves.

It is an astonishing power that He gives us. Our freedom is an impossibly great gift, and if we are not careful, we end up using it in such a way that we condemn ourselves as harshly as the devil condemns us. We either stand in the freedom wherewith Christ has set us free, or we stand with Satan—which is the Hebrew word for "Accuser"—condemning and accusing God, and thereby condemning and accusing ourselves.

Jesus tells us these things to warn us, and has given us this parable in that vein. We are so free that if we do not see our freedom and live it out, we make ourselves slaves. Not just slaves to sin, but slaves to the one who wishes to drag us into the eternal slavery of Hell.

And there is no middle way. We sink or we swim. We either step out of the boat and miraculously walk on the water to Jesus, or we drown. As it happens, we cannot remain in the boat. And those who do remain in the boat will drown as surely as the one who has stepped out of the boat and does not walk to Jesus upon the water.

Chapter Fourteen

Justifying Ourselves

To attempt to justify ourselves before God is to wish to be God ourselves, which never ends well. And whenever we do this we fall into the trap of behaving in a "religious" way—which is to say we are actually falling into the trap of moralism.

In the same way we pretend we can fool God by donning a fig leaf to cover our nakedness, or by pointing at a creed to say what we believe, we mean to cynically use a "religious" excuse. We pretend this is the safe path, just as the servant who has buried the talent pretends he is taking the safe path, but is really condemning his master as being hard. His lie is a religious lie.

But in all these cases we imagine we know that God is a hard judge, and we deal with Him as such. We cover ourselves with fig leaves and claim to believe certain creeds, or we say that we buried the talent so we wouldn't lose it. But God sees our deeper motivation is satanic. It is to supplant Him and become Him ourselves. We attempt to manipulate Him with our actions so that it is we who are in charge and not God Himself. This is the path of dead religion, and religious scrupulosity is at its heart. The Pharisees would tithe their mint and other herbs, but their hearts were far from God.

But when we treat God as the hard judge in the parable, it is obvious we are living in fear of Him. We do not love Him but secretly hate Him. We believe that if we make the slightest mistake He will condemn us, so we do as little as possible (bury the talent) and certainly avoid any kind of sin or action we think wrong. But by living in this way we cease to live freely. We are in bondage.

In Bonhoeffer's time, many in the Church had taken this path. They avoided trouble. For one thing they cooperated with the authorities, because Romans 13 seemed to make that unavoidable. It was not their job to argue with those authorities or resist them—and certainly not to work against them. They must be good citizens and let things happen as they happened.

But Bonhoeffer in his essay "The Church and the Jewish Question" made it clear it is very much the Church's obligation to counter the state if the state's actions are evil. God was calling His people to something far above merely avoiding sins and keeping their noses clean.

For most in the German Church, God was the "hard master" of the parable whom they feared and disliked. So their actions were calculated to give Him back His talent and be done with it. But Bonhoeffer clearly saw this was not merely wrong, but evil. It was not merely that the churchgoers of his day did not love God, but actually hated him. The difference between these views may be summed up by saying, "Being a Christian is not about avoiding sin, but about passionately and courageously serving God."

So why *do* some keep silent at certain times or avoid certain subjects? Is it because they are afraid of making a mistake for which God will judge them? Many in the Church today have what Bonhoeffer might have called "theologically restrained objections" to coming across as political, or even merely to voting for a candidate whose demeanor doesn't tick all the boxes they think necessary. For them, it is not about doing what they think is the right thing for all concerned—whether in how they vote or in other things—but is more about their own theological purity. In other words, they are not thinking about others, but about themselves. But they are doing it for "religious" or "pietistic" reasons.

✠

Let's take the example of a Gestapo officer coming to the door of a man hiding a Jew in his basement. Perhaps the homeowner is a good citizen who "doesn't want any trouble," but who, when the desperate Jew came to him, was not able to turn him away. He may have been afraid that someone would see him talking to the Jew, and perhaps it was safer to let him hide in his basement for a while than risk being seen talking to him. Of course the Jew could not stay there, but for the moment, it was the best option.

But now comes the moment of truth. A Gestapo officer comes up the man's walk and knocks on his door. The man answers and the Gestapo agent puts the question to him unadorned: "Are you hiding a Jew in your basement?" But wait, perhaps the Gestapo agent is craftier than that. He doesn't wish to implicate the homeowner in this, and perhaps nudge him to lie. On the contrary, he wishes to show the homeowner that if he plays along with the government—whom he, the Gestapo agent, represents—then it will go well. After all, the homeowner is not himself a Jew. So perhaps the Gestapo agent asks: "Has a Jew imposed himself upon you, and is hiding in your basement?" If that is the case, the homeowner is as much a victim as anyone. The Gestapo is there to help.

So the man has to make a decision. He goes to church and knows that lying is a sin—or so he has always understood. If he says there is no Jew in his basement, he will be guilty of lying; not only will he be in trouble with the Gestapo and perhaps be sent to a concentration camp, but he will be guilty before God, too. He must never lie! What would God make of it if he did? So to be justified before God—to be sinless in this matter—he tells the Gestapo agent what he knows as a fact. "Yes, indeed," he says, relieved. "There is a Jew in our basement."

In his book *Ethics*, Bonhoeffer gives the example of a young girl in school, whom the teacher harshly asks, "Is your father a drunkard?" Bonhoeffer explains that in this case the girl does not owe the teacher any answer. She does not owe the teacher the "truth" of the matter because the plain facts of it and the actual truth of it are two different things. She is under no obligation to dishonor her parents and give this prying teacher the dirty piece of information he wishes to ferret from her in the name of "truth." So if she does not answer or even if she says no, Bonhoeffer says she is justified. Her "lie" is not the sort of lie even God would condemn. Far from it.

The homeowner in whose basement the Jew is hiding is in a similar situation. The Gestapo agent wishes to harm—or just as likely murder—the Jew. So the agent does not represent God, and any answer to his question must reflect the reality at hand. But if the homeowner views God as a "hard master," his answer will not serve the truth. It will serve neither justice nor God's purposes; it will serve the devil's purposes. So if the homeowner tries to justify himself by "not lying" in answering this question, he delivers the Jew to his torturers, but feels it was the only option he had. After all, he could not lie, could he?

But again, God takes another view. God is not a moralistic fuss-budget or nitpicking God who is lying in wait. When we tell a lie for a larger good, He does not swoop in and say "Aha!" and condemn us. If we know who God truly is, we know that He is not against us, but for us. He is not Satan the accuser, looking for what sins He can find to condemn us. He is the gracious and loving God who sent His own Son to die so that we could be forgiven and saved. And when He sees us act in a way that is not calculated to protect ourselves but that is rather magnanimous and self-sacrificing for the sake of another, He rejoices—because in this He sees that we know Him to be not the hard master, but our loving Father in Heaven.

So for example, if we vote for someone whom others may criticize as being guilty of this or that, the real question is, did we vote for that candidate because we genuinely believed they would enact policies to help people, despite what some might think? Or did we vote or not vote because we were mostly concerned about what others would think of us? Were we thinking of ourselves, or were we thinking of others? These are the questions we must answer honestly.

Let me further illustrate my point.

The Story of Rahab

In the Book of Joshua we have the story of the two spies whom Joshua sends to Jericho, which God has commanded him to conquer. They go to the home of a prostitute named Rahab, who hides them. It is similar to the fictional story of the Gestapo agent we have just told. Rahab not only hides the Israelite spies, but when the king of Jericho sends his men to her house, she lies, saying that they have left—which they certainly have not.

We might think she was only doing this to save herself and her family, knowing that the Israelites were blessed by God and would certainly overtake Jericho. But even in this, we mistake the larger meaning. The author makes it quite plain that because she knew the God of the Israelites was truly God—and was with the Israelites—her actions are considered the actions of a woman of faith. That she is a prostitute who lies only underscores the point for us. If we think of God as a hard master and moralistic judge mostly concerned with whether we "sin" or not, we have missed the point and do not know God at all. A hard master and moralistic judge could never count a prostitute as worthy of his praise and blessing. That God is not God, but the devil. He is legalistically scrupulous on such issues, and certainly could not reward this woman for openly lying.

But as we say, the God of the Bible is not quite who we think He is. Of course He is against prostitution and against lying, but He is far more against those who are moralists and legalists because He knows they do not know Him. They do not know Him as a loving God, and therefore they do not love Him. In fact, they hate Him. So because of Rahab's faith in the God of Israel, she is lauded both in James's letter and in Hebrews 11, the famous "Hall of Faith."

But it goes much farther than that.

For context, we should know that the spies who went to Jericho might well have chosen Rahab's home to visit precisely because she was a prostitute, knowing this would be a place their presence would be easier to keep secret. But by standing boldly with the people of Israel—with the people of God—Rahab somehow stood with God Himself. So when Jericho was destroyed, not only was she not killed, but—according to the Scriptures—she actually lived with the Israelites for the remainder of her days. We must know they would not have allowed her to continue in her profession. So the only conclusion we can draw is that her act of faith—for such it is called twice in the New Testament—enabled her to find complete forgiveness and redemption, so much so that God enabled her to be in the very genealogy of the Messiah of the world. It is an astonishing story and a perfect picture of the boundless mercy of the God of the Bible.

Can we imagine that we find Rahab's name in the genealogy of Jesus? The God of grace and love is a God of such redemption as we can hardly fathom. He reaches out in love to anyone, and especially to those who know they are not respectable, who are not fooled into thinking they are somehow justified by their own behavior. So if our own view of God is too constricted and constipated to see that He reaches out to those whom we might loathe and think beneath us, we only condemn ourselves.

✳

The picture we have now is of a God who is not the pinched and moralistic religious deity some have painted him to be, but rather of a God who has a wildness and unpredictability to Him. We may remember that in C. S. Lewis's *Chronicles of Narnia*, we learn that Aslan—the Christ figure of those extraordinary books—is not tame, but wild. And he is good. But the goodness of God is a wild and unpredictable goodness, infinitely far from the pious and "religious" tameness so many of us have mistaken for the real thing.

After all, He is himself a Person and not a set of rules or an algorithm. The Jesus who confounded the elite religious leaders of His day—but who made the simple crowds cheer—is that God. To those who worshiped that "religious" God of their own making, who was not God at all, what Jesus said was infuriating and what He did enraging, which is why they knew they must kill Him. And in allowing them to do this, He infuriated and enraged them once and for all eternity, for in this way He defeated Death itself. It is this glorious Jesus—wild and unpredictable—who reveals Himself to us now and calls us to follow Him. Dare we do anything less? Shall we not trust Him? Will we trust Him? We were created to do that very thing, so to do anything less is to fearfully writhe away from the magnificent freedom He gives us and to find ourselves forever in chains.

Chapter Fifteen

"Religionless Christianity"

For freedom Christ has set us free; stand firm therefore, and do
not submit again to a yoke of slavery.

—*GALATIANS 5:1*

Paul's words to the Galatian church should haunt us, because there can be no question that we in the American Church have drifted from the pure and utter freedom that it means to live out our faith fearlessly. Will we repent of this and avoid the sure judgment that comes of our disobedience? Or will we continue to let fear dictate what we do, and continue in our religious bondage to sin and death, and reap the whirlwind?

Bonhoeffer had been calling the German Church to this kind of freedom and faith, but in vain. He knew that few had heard what God was saying through him, and that he had been misunderstood by most—many of whom would nonetheless survive him and see for themselves the rightness of what he had been saying.

But without question the most misunderstood thing in all of Bonhoeffer's life came after his death, when confused, theologically liberal theologians seized on two words he had written in a private letter to his friend Eberhard Bethge. Bonhoeffer never dreamt the world would see the letter, but Bethge was persuaded after his friend's death to publish his letters, which were filled with profound and important thoughts. The book was titled *Letters and Papers from Prison*. But in the post-war confusion, a false narrative arose as a result, claiming that Bonhoeffer in his final days had drifted away from the theologically orthodox Christianity so evident in his earlier writings and had slowly evolved toward a kind of humanist position in which the God of the Scriptures was no longer at issue—as though the Bonhoeffer in the dank solitude of his prison cells had reconsidered everything and had come out in a different place than the Bonhoeffer of the previous decade. As it happens, this was untrue in every way; indeed, precisely the opposite was true. But many times, a false narrative takes hold, and decades or centuries may pass before it is corrected.

Bonhoeffer was indeed reconsidering everything in the solitude of his prison cells, but the way in which he did so and the results were perfectly opposed to what many confused post-war theologians had so hastily and sloppily concluded. In his letter to Bethge, Bonhoeffer wondered whether we needed a "religionless Christianity"; he was not saying we need a religion devoid of Christianity or apart from Christianity, but exactly the opposite. He was saying we need a true and a deep Christianity, one that is not merely "religious," one that does not lie to God with "fig leaves" of theological statements and creeds, but that understands we are to live out our faith with every atom of our being in every second we have on this earth, and with every breath God gives us to breathe. Anything less than this kind of faith is nothing at all.

Bonhoeffer saw it was the dead religion of German Lutheranism of that time that had failed to stand against the unprecedented evil of the Nazis, just as he had warned in his Reformation Day sermon in 1932. Bonhoeffer saw what had happened, and in his private letter to his best friend, he said as much. He knew more surely than ever that the days of mere church attendance and intellectual assent to various doctrines were the culprits, that they were what had allowed the unprecedented evils of that time to flourish. The dead religion of many churches in Germany had shown itself not only to be flimsy and useless, but to be piously playing the part assigned it by the devil himself. The "Christianity" of the German churches had been dead religion masquerading as Christianity, and in succumbing to it, those churches had become nothing less than handmaidens of evil. Bonhoeffer saw that if evil ever were to come again, it would require nothing less than a true faith, a "religionless Christianity" that would stand with everything against that evil, that would give it no quarter, and that by the grace of the God who had died for us would triumph to His glory.

It is ironic and tragic that Bonhoeffer in his prophetic way was unable to communicate these things to the German Church before it was too late, and it is further ironic and tragic that when the rubble was settling over the ruins of Europe, his nearly final words on the larger subject were so widely and fundamentally misunderstood. But the question comes to us in the American Church all these years later: Will we heed Bonhoeffer's cry for a full-throated faith that does not hope, but that *knows* God has defeated death, and that lives in a way that makes this plain to anyone who cares to see? Will we kick away the traces of our dead religiosity and fear-based pieties and speak truth whenever we have that opportunity, come what may? Will we wipe away the false boundaries between our faith and everything else—whether "politics" or culture—and act as though Truth is a Person who knows no bounds, who created the heavens and the earth and all that is in them, and who died that we who are the crowns of God's creation might at last live in true freedom, with the authority that He gave us when He died and rose from the grave?

We have come to that place in history now, and the Lord looks to us, the American Church. Will we be His people now, as the world looks to us in the midst of madness? Our Bible studies and sermons have all been meaningless if we do not make what we learned come alive in ways that are self-sacrificial and that show we really do know that God has defeated death. To do anything less than this is to represent a lie, and to lie to God in doing so. How else shall we put it? This is the hour for which each of us has been born. If we live fully in that freedom for which Christ has set us free, we will see God's hand in ways we dare not imagine. We will see miracles small and great, and we will see not only revival, but reformation. We will see the goodness of God make its way into everything we do, because that is God's will for us and for the world at this time. Many who do not yet know the God we claim to worship will see how we live and will want to know Him, and will come to know Him, and will become a part of what He is doing in our generation. Dare we believe that, or are we already headed to the caves, believing nothing we do can matter, and that judgment is falling and all we can do is save ourselves?

So you who are the Church—for it is not an institution, but a collection of each of us, in direct personal relationship to God—are responsible in this. *You.* It does not happen apart from you and cannot happen apart from you. God looks to you now, and to you alone. He has put history and the future in your hands. In the end, you cannot look to your pastors or leaders, but must look to God Himself. He will lead you in this, and you will either let Him lead you, or you will not succeed. He created you for a relationship with Himself, and although He wishes to use your pastors and leaders in helping you along this journey, He cannot do so unless you yourself take the ultimate responsibility in this. It is with you that He wants a deep and a personal relationship. He created you for that, and your life can never be what it is meant to be unless you know that and step into it without fear.

Are you willing? Are you ready? God has chosen each of us to live now, at this very moment in history, for His eternal purposes. We are not here now by some mistake. God has ordained that we be born when we were born and that we live now, to do the works now that He has prepared for us in advance, to His glory. It is an unimaginable privilege. This is the hour of the American Church. We are charged with pointing our fellow Americans and the whole world to the God who has somehow allowed us the inexpressibly great privilege of representing Him in these dark days. Will we do so? Will you?

But sometimes, in order to do something, we need to see an example of it. As my friend B. J. Weber has often asked, "What would that look like?" And so, for a final example of what this might look like, we turn to something that happened in 1987.

Chapter Sixteen

The Final Push

Mr. Gorbachev, tear down this wall!

—*RONALD REAGAN*

It was June 1987. President Ronald Reagan was visiting what was then West Berlin, and was to give a speech at the historic Brandenburg Gate adjacent to the infamous Berlin Wall. It was the most vivid and monstrous symbol of Communism in the world, separating East Berlin from West Berlin, and of course was erected to keep those in East Berlin from escaping to the free west. Imagine a society so inhuman that it must erect a literal wall to keep its people from escaping. Of course, this is what evil must always do. It must cancel voices that speak against it, and must kill those who stand against it, and must imprison those who might escape its reach.

Ronald Reagan was an exceedingly rare leader in that he was fierce and bold in speaking out against the great evil of Communism, and genuinely wanted to bring it down, to bring freedom to its captives, if God might use him to do that. But what made Reagan even rarer as a leader was that he seemed to understand that the Soviet regime was weak. It had always pretended to be strong, and to be inevitable and permanent. And many world leaders—including many in America, from both parties—had seemed to believe this lie. But Reagan seemed to know that because the Soviet Union was built on a lie, it was unsustainable and could be brought down—if someone had the courage to stand and fight against it. Which brings us to the single and magnificently memorable line he delivered that day as he stood there, framed visually by the Brandenburg Gate. It came in the middle of the speech, as he courageously and unexpectedly addressed the ugly reality of the infamous wall so close to where he stood. It was the proverbial elephant in the world's living room, and suddenly Reagan would dare to address it. It was an extraordinary moment.

Most American leaders had been diffident about confronting the Soviets head on in these things. During the Nixon administration, under the Secretary of State Henry Kissinger, the idea of "detente," which referred to the de-escalation of hostilities, had ruled the day. Kissinger also had often invoked the term "Realpolitik," which was a fancy way of saying that one must accept things as they are and not try too hard to change the status quo. Was this cynical, or was it cowardly? Or was it simply realistic?

In any event, in 1980—not long before Reagan was elected—the Soviet Union had invaded Afghanistan, showing that perhaps "detente" was not so effective after all. The Soviets had shown themselves more than eager to take advantage of any opportunities that presented themselves to expand their empire. At that time Jimmy Carter was president, and the weakness he projected during his time in office made it difficult for the Soviets not to take advantage of the situation.

Indeed it was doubtless Carter's failures that led to Reagan's election, and so, from the beginning of Reagan's presidency—as throughout his career—he would confront the evil of the Soviets and of Communism directly. But in 1987, in the weeks before his famous Brandenburg speech, when conferring with his advisers, Reagan had brought up his desire to say this famous line—"Mr. Gorbachev, tear down this wall!"—and all of the establishment figures around him had expressed their serious disapproval.

Chief of Staff Howard Baker scowled that it would be "extreme" and "unpresidential," and General Colin Powell—then Reagan's deputy national security adviser—had soberly agreed. As far as they were concerned, such a direct and bold challenge to the head of the Soviet Union could only inflame the tensions between East and West.

It's always challenging to argue with the worldly wisdom of such as Baker, Powell, and Kissinger. But truly great leaders know that sometimes doing the heroic and right thing is a lonely business, and that they will probably never get those around them to understand what they are doing. This is one of the hallmarks of true leadership. As we have said, Bonhoeffer felt quite alone in what he was doing, but he did it anyway, knowing that he had to be concerned only with the audience of One, who was God. And in 1987, Reagan knew that he could not do what the established "diplomatic" voices were demanding he do. Like Bonhoeffer, he knew that history would judge him and that God would judge him for what he did. And like Wilberforce, who thought of the Africans in slave ships, Reagan thought of those in the vast network of the Soviet gulag, many of whom had been cruelly persecuted for their Christian faith by the atheist Communist regime. Was there no one out there in the free world who really believed it was worth at least trying to deliver them from their suffering?

Of course, one cannot help but suspect that establishment figures like Baker and Powell—like so many Republicans today, and so many in the American Church today—were in fact comfortable with the status quo. Often in history, leaders think of something as a "necessary evil" that cannot be vanquished and are only too happy to stand aside and let it continue, as though trying to bring it down is naïve and foolish. Most in Wilberforce's day thought of the slave trade this way. To go against such things was to tilt at windmills. But Reagan—like so many great leaders—was willing to come across as wild and unpredictable in how he led, if that was necessary. He was certainly sickened by the fathomless evil of the Soviet Union and refused simply to see it as inevitable "status quo." He clearly wanted to do anything he could to bring down what just four years earlier he had infamously called "the Evil Empire," which was another example of what his critics saw as his impolitic approach.

So Reagan was not about to let those around him dissuade him from saying what he clearly felt must be said in West Berlin that day. The world would be watching. And so that day, he said it, and with steel in his voice delivered the now famous line—"Mr. Gorbachev, tear down this wall!"

And when he said it, something happened. It was as though those words were more than words and carried tremendous spiritual power. Because when he spoke them, a crack began to appear in what so many had thought of as an adamantine edifice. It was as though with the single deft and well-aimed blow of those words, the world changed. People suffering in Soviet prisons would hear about it and would tap about it through the walls to each other. Someone out there, far away from them, knew about them and was fighting for them. Someone out there cared enough to boldly speak against the evil that imprisoned them and millions of other fellow sufferers. Someone out there believed in truth and freedom and was not afraid to fight for these ideals. We can hardly imagine how much hope that one line delivered to prisoners around the world.

Although Reagan hardly thought of it as such, what he said was a kind of prophetic declaration. Can we doubt that apparatchiks across the Soviet Union—not to mention demons—trembled when he delivered that line, when they realized that there was someone who had seen through their lies and who was on to them? What he said proclaimed liberty to the captives—literally and figuratively. It had tremendous power, as words sometimes can have. Reagan did what no one had done before, and in time the whole Berlin Wall—and then the so-called "Iron Curtain"—would come down. The vast seven-decades-old Soviet Empire would collapse, never to rise again. What he said paved the way for all that followed, and as we now know, in 1989, the Berlin Wall was toppled—and two years later the Soviet Union itself was dissolved. It is one of the greatest miracles in history, and what Reagan said that day was among the most important things that made it possible.

When we think of what he said that day, we might think of David going up against Goliath as hundreds of Israelite soldiers cowered. David knew that he couldn't defeat the giant by himself, but he knew that God was with him. And as a result, we have been talking about what he did for three millennia. It is these people and these actions that change the world. All of the diplomatic niceties so strongly advised by the Bakers and the Powells of the world cannot understand it and cannot see that in the "safe" approach of their worldly wisdom, they are in fact aiding and abetting evil. It seems that they only want to keep it at bay indefinitely and never actually engage with it in open warfare, instead simply preferring to stay out of its way. But David and Wilberforce and Bonhoeffer and Reagan and others—who are outraged by the evil that they see—are willing to risk everything to engage it, and to fight with all their might and main, whatever the outcome. They know that unless they try to vanquish it, evil will win.

What does this mean to us today? Is there something that to many of us now seems invincible and immovable, as the Iron Curtain and the Soviet empire seemed invincible and immovable? As the slave trade and slavery once did? Is there something that frightens us enough that we believe it ought not to be directly countered, but that rather ought to be pacified so that we might coexist with it? And what is this thing, if it exists in our time? What do so many perhaps wish might go away but many fear never will, so that we must make peace with it? Is it the cultural Marxism that talks about systemic racism, or the transgender madness that says the Bible's view of human beings and sexuality is completely false, and is actually harmful and must be destroyed?

We know the Soviet Union was the face of atheistic Communism, but what we face today is rather less simple to see. What we face is not a nation state that imprisons its citizens within its walls, but it forwards the ideology of atheist Marxism nonetheless and probably does so even more effectively. Many think it is a precursor of what has been described as the system of anti-Christ—and whether it is or is not, it certainly stands against Christ and what we read in the Bible.

But the only question we need ask is: What would God have us do? If He be for us, who can be against us? Is our faith that kind of faith? We cheer for David, but dare we go up against the Goliath of our time? Or would we rather shrink back into the ranks of the Israelite soldiers as everyone else? Of course David—albeit imperfect and quite human—was a type of Christ. And armed with real faith in the Lord of Hosts, he did what no one else could do, and slayed the giant who had cursed God's people and God Himself.

✳

Reagan knew that the Soviet Union presented itself—as all bullies and monsters and devils do—as something more powerful than it was. He knew that what its leaders desperately feared was that someone like himself would call their bluff. And he knew that most of the people around him had been perfectly content not to call that bluff, but to be bluffed. He—along with Margaret Thatcher in England and Pope John

Paul II—knew that if they three fought hard, and pushed with everything they had, they could forever vanquish the "Evil Empire" that was the Soviet Union. And now we know that they did just that.

But before it happened, they were denounced as unrealistic and as anti-Communist "extremists." Nearly everyone but the three of them behaved as though the Soviet Union really were like an impenetrable and permanent wall that must be accepted and never be touched. But these three had the idea that it was a false wall. And that if they all with a concerted effort gave it a good shove, it would reveal itself to be a sham—a weak and tottering facade whose main posts were rotten. It would go down. Which was why those in power in the Soviet Union—who really knew it to be weak and on the brink of collapse—had to do everything they could to pretend it was immovable and permanent. But those with eyes to see knew this was a lie and knew that they must do what all the worldly wisdom said never to do. By the grace of God, they did it. And the wall came a-tumbling down.

So the question comes to us. Will we all together now push that false barrier that stands so tall and so long that we cannot see over it and cannot see the end of it? Will we trust God who tells us that victory will be given into our hands and that we must fight with all we have? Or will we, like the twelve thousand pastors in Germany, hang back and see which way the wind is blowing, and in our inaction guarantee that evil prevails? Will we let the three thousand do all the work, watch them fail, and rejoice that we weren't foolish enough to join them in their foolhardy crusade?

God is clearly calling us not to do that, not to repeat the unspeakably grievous errors of the Christians of that time. But He cannot and will not force us to do what is right. He only warns us and gives us the chilling example of what happened the last time, and through Bonhoeffer and others exhorts us to do what is right. Will we? Will you?

Heaven looks to you and to me to do the right thing. What part of the tottering wall has God called you to push? Are you to run for office? To homeschool your children? To give millions to some vital cause for freedom and truth and justice? Are you to speak out in a situation where others are being silent? Are you to vote—and even advocate—for a candidate some are denouncing as "un-Christian", but whom you nonetheless know to be a champion of God's purposes? Are you to risk your job—or your congregation, or something else? God is looking to see whether you trust Him with it, whatever it is. He is waiting for you to show Him that you know that whatever you have is His gift to you, and that you can trust Him with it.

As we have said, to do what God asks always takes a certain amount of wildness. We remember that God is good, but His goodness is not safe and it is not tame. God is not the religious God of the Pharisees. He does not call us to be tame or safe or religious. It's safer to bury the talent, but God condemns us when we behave in that way. It's safer to hang back and see which way the wind blows—but God condemns us for hanging back when He has called us to the battle.

Bonhoeffer once told a student that every sermon should have a "shot of heresy" in it. Of course, this didn't mean that Bonhoeffer was advocating actual heresy, but he was calling attention to something that we see in the life of Jesus, who over and over shows us the unpredictability and wildness in the goodness of God, which challenges our safe religious pieties. When we follow Him in this way, we are certain to be misunderstood by those who cling to their safe pieties and "worldly wisdom." When they see the kind of behavior that Jesus exhibited—and that David and Bonhoeffer and Wilberforce and Reagan and so many others have exhibited—they will clutch their pearls and lift their skirts and express their horror at it. They have always done this. The Pharisees did it when Jesus said most of what He said. The twelve thousand pastors did it when Bonhoeffer went out on a limb in following God where no one else was willing to follow. And the establishment has done it in American politics and in American churches, and has blanched when someone shows real leadership and a real willingness to fight against evil. We cannot help but assume they have no idea of what Jesus was saying in the Parable of the Talents and are convinced that the wisest path really was to bury the talent and simply to keep one's head down and stay out of trouble.

But again, the question comes not to them, but to you. Will you be the leader that God has called you to be in this way? Will you follow Him wherever He goes, and be a true disciple by looking to Him alone in what you say and do? If a holy remnant will now do that—and exhort others to join them—we will see such things in Heaven and Earth as were never dreamt of in your philosophy, Horatio. We will see God's hand move in our time, for His purposes. We will see God's will be done on Earth as it is in Heaven. Amen.